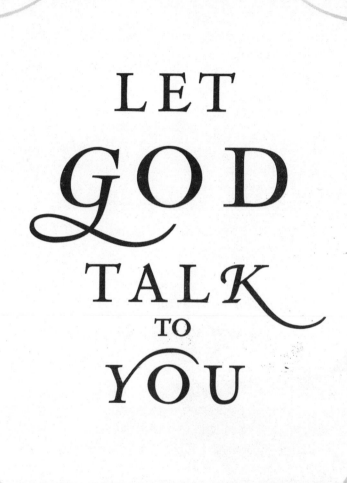

LET

GOD

TALK

TO

YOU

When You Hear Him,

You Will Never Be the Same

BECKY TIRABASSI

LET GOD TALK TO YOU

BETHANY HOUSE PUBLISHERS

Minneapolis, Minnesota

ACKNOWLEDGMENTS

In every author's life there are family, friends, and a team of people who offer to take an idea and help turn it into a book that will ultimately change people's lives for the better, even forever.

I'm very fortunate to have a family who not only gives me the time and space to write for hours on end, but who graciously allows me to tell their stories. Thank you, Roger, Jake, and Khara Tirabassi, Rick Hunter, Reg Mantei, and Mom for caring so deeply about me and for God.

I also have a fabulous group of friends. A few of them volunteered to be my writer's group for *Let God Talk to You*. During the many winter months in which I wrote this book, they daily returned submissions within hours (and sometimes minutes) of receiving them, keeping me focused and on deadline. This was an incredible gift to me. Thank you, Matt Mancinelli, Brenda Haan, Kathy Nunamaker, and (again) Reg Mantei for caring about this book and its readers.

Finally, I want to thank the entire team of publishing professionals who have made this a better book by relentlessly asking me challenging questions and expecting the highest standards of me, especially Bob Zaloba of GRQ, and Ellen Chalifoux and Kyle Duncan of Bethany House.

CONTENTS

Let God Talk to You

The first time I heard God talk to me, I ended a six-year relationship with alcohol—instantly. I remember exactly where I was and what day and year it was. I'm one of those people who is convinced that once you hear God talk, you'll never be the same.

In that first conversation, God proved to me that He talks *and* listens not only to those who know Him well, but to even the sickest soul.

Since that day, God most often talks to me through His Word, followed by simple thoughts or ideas—requiring some action, often very practical, but not necessarily easy to do. At first, what He asks of me may seem unusual, or even impossible. However, if I don't argue or procrastinate and willingly follow His directions, His voice gets clearer and clearer. In fact, His voice almost always stirs some emotion in me: my heart races, my cheeks flood with redness, or my toes tap quickly and anxiously until I do or say what I feel He is compelling me to do or say.

When God talks to me, I always feel motivated—physically, emotionally, or spiritually. Whether gentle or bold, His words give me courage to do or say something, to stop or to start something, most often to help someone else.

I've learned that it isn't very smart to ignore God when He talks to me. When I don't listen to Him, I lose my way and hurt myself, or worse, I hurt someone else.

Numerous times each day, God talks to me, and others will indeed confirm that it is God talking! For example, when I tell others what I've heard God say, their eyes give me feedback. They often cry spontaneously, or their wide-open eyes confirm they agree with what I've just said. Many times they simply lower their gaze so as not to look me directly in the eye—they're either ashamed or embarrassed or pensive. Their eyes tell me that what I have said resonates with their pain or feelings or emotions—something I wouldn't have known about them, something only God knows.

Of course I love it when God talks to me in those "mountaintop" moments, when an explosion of clarity, purpose, and then unrestrained emotion erupts within me. In those moments I feel so ready to change, so empowered and full of hope. Yet as anticlimactic as it sounds, it's after the emotion has dissipated and reality has set in that I'm *most* convinced I have indeed heard God speak.

God talks to me in a variety of ways—always through His written Word, consistently throughout the day by touching my heart or prompting me with a thought, and sometimes even through silence. His voice is so distinct that I've made a habit of writing down immediately what I think or feel He's saying. Over the years, day after day, my handwritten, two-way conversations with God are black-and-white proof that He knows me so very well, so deeply, and He still loves me! His unconditional love keeps me coming back to hear what He has to say.

In all honesty, there are times when I feel a pull, as if something wants to distract me, to lure me away from my "God Talks." In those moments, I have to fight for my time alone with God or those minutes will quickly vanish, only to be consumed by some urgent interruption.

I've learned to recognize when God talks to me. And if I listen intentionally for Him, I'll hear almost a whisper, then a more distinct impression that draws me toward Him, until I am certain it is God talking. It is always at that juncture that I must make a decision with all of my heart, body, soul, and mind to believe it is His voice and not my thoughts that I am hearing. When I let my faith respond to the sound of God's voice, I get "fired up" and "filled up," empowered and courageous and committed to leave our two-way conversations, ready to change the world.

I just know that if you really believe God wants to talk to you, that He holds in His heart all the answers to your questions, that He is always as close as your thoughts, that He loves you just the way you are, that He waits for you to wake up in the morning—you will not only hear Him, but find Him to be your greatest source of strength and encouragement. For these reasons and many more, I have written *Let God Talk to You*.

CHAPTER 1

God Talks to Anyone!

God talks.
    He does.

God Talks to Those Who Are Desperate

A friend's daughter is desperately ill. She doesn't have much hope, say the doctors. She is a victim of an unknown bacterium that is ravaging her body. I've been by her bedside when her father stands over her and *boldly* pours out his heart and soul to God. He doesn't hold back. He doesn't fear the worst. He hopes for the miraculous, in spite of the doctors' reports. He believes that God is able to do anything at anytime for anyone. So he asks God to help. Unashamed, he begs, knowing he talks to a loving Father.

His demeanor and confidence suggest that he indeed hears God talk to him—for he keeps fighting, believing, and speaking words of hope over his daughter. The visitors—of both small and great faith—follow the father's lead. They too talk to God on behalf of this young girl and wait for God to respond. There is no formula, just sincere pleading and often deep wailing.

Yet God talks. How? He gives noticeable courage to a severely tested family. He strengthens the fatigued parents. He keeps the daughter's heart beating, the air moving in and out of her nose and lungs. Her blood keeps flowing. A faint smile on her face speaks volumes as it grows more vibrant with each passing week. Her "thumbs up" in answer to questions, her closed eyes when someone offers a prayer, suggest daily progress.

With each new day, with each new obstacle to overcome, the family gathers the next-step options and discusses them with God. Then they wait for God to talk to them by giving them confidence to move in a specific direction. They don't make a move until they sense His peace in their hearts and minds. They keep listening for God to speak.

These parents understand that no amount of money, education, or medicine can stop an unknown bacterium, restore a battered heart and brain, or replay a twenty-four-hour period and magically edit out the bad parts. Only God can do something that impossible. Only God can carry them through every valley and over every mountain. So they attentively listen for God to give them His thoughts, His ideas, and His encouraging words—especially when almost every other word they hear is negative. They hold on to God's words—written in their Bible, emblazoned in their hearts, whispered in their minds.

Dependent and desperate, the parents continuously and courageously call out to God—waiting, expectant. They ask *Him* to talk to them and to the doctors, to help their daughter, to do the impossible. They are sustained by His powerful, strong voice.

People who are hopeless *want* God to talk to them. They *want* to hear the good news that is able to lift them out of the overwhelming despair in which they are drowning.

Truly desperate people don't ignore or underestimate the supernatural. *They seek it*. They don't critically analyze what *others* have said about God or waste precious time thoughtfully considering what *they* believe about God. Their gut reaction, their immediate response—if they are truly at the end of their resources—is to call upon God's name and ask Him for help. They may shout at the top of their lungs, as if to reach the sky: *"God, help me. Help us. God . . . please. Please, God, talk to me. Do something!"*

Expectant people hear God speak—whether they are fully devoted followers of His or strangers to His name.

I know. That is how my first encounter with God unfolded.

After a series of the most self-destructive events imaginable, I—a young woman whose party life abruptly turned into something much more dangerous—heard God speak.

At the time, I wasn't in a position of favor or even friendship with God. I didn't acknowledge His existence. I certainly didn't love Him, worship Him, or follow Him. No, I was running from God, even though I had heard much about Him during my childhood. And if He *was* real, I had nothing but shame to offer Him.

Then on my most despairing day, in a suicidal moment, I racked my brain, riffling through any possible reasons for living or just one idea that could keep me alive for one more day. But the most consuming thought in my head was the suggestion to end my life. I kept pushing it away as a last resort, hoping to find some way—*any* other way—to escape my self-inflicted pain. I became more and more afraid that I was looking for an impossible solution.

I was desperate, to be sure—but not for religion.

I had been raised in a time when religious traditions were readily exchanged for unconventional attitudes about sexual experimentation and all methods of self-indulgence. The latter fit me perfectly. The youth movement of the 1970s offered unbridled freedom and captured the imagination of many students in my generation, and I became one of its most avid followers. As I pursued an unscripted, pleasure-seeking path, it took only six years before I completely lost my grasp on reality. I threw away my education, ties to family, work ethic, morals, childhood faith, and any thread of self-respect.

From that most ugly pit, which included addiction to drugs, sex, and alcohol, I looked up and called out God's name. Not in a church service or under the guidance of clergy; instead I found myself in a hallway, talking to a janitor who found me in tears after a drunk-driving court hearing. His advice? Talk to God.

What should have sounded like a radical—even repulsive—idea to someone as irreligious as myself, seemed both inviting and vaguely familiar.

Without much hesitation, out loud and in front of this stranger, I told God, like a remorseful child might break down in front of her loving father, that I was sorry for—everything. Then I asked God to just help me live, to change me.

Desperate is a word that describes those who have no recourse; they can't find their way out of a hole or a mess or a dead end. And very often they have arrived at their destination of hopelessness with only themselves to blame. They have no other options, no Plan B. No one even cares about them anymore. Their well has run dry. Their time has run out. They are alone in the world. And they are the first to admit they deserve nothing.

When God talks to a hopeless person, here is what He says (at least this is what I heard Him say to me):

"I'm right here. I hear you calling me. I see your tears. It's time to stop running toward who or what will never satisfy you or fill your emptiness. I am the one you are looking for. I am all you need. Turn to me. I'm right here ready to catch you, wanting to hold you. I love you very much, more than you can even understand right now. And I forgive you for everything. Yes, everything. I am yours, always and forever. Put your hand in mine. Put your hope in me. Come to me now. Don't be afraid. Just come."

How do I know it was God talking? It started with a feeling, but it turned into some compelling, overpowering, and straightforward thoughts.

I heard someone talk to me—not audibly, but from outside of me—with words that were comforting and full of compassion. For years I was desperate to possess these feelings, but I couldn't muster them up no matter how hard I tried. For months previously I had been consumed with guilt—twenty-four hours a day. But as if to immediately wash away my shame, I felt a liquid, hot love being poured over me. Simultaneously I felt forgiven and hope-filled.

For weeks prior I could not even look at or talk to those around me without seeing disappointment displayed on their faces or hearing it in their voices. But in this most desperate moment, I heard God speak *kindly* to me. And though I didn't see His face, I could feel His love.

God was convincing me that I was lovable, that my life was worth living. *I just knew these weren't my own thoughts or emotions. No one loved me.* But the thoughts were unstoppable and accompanied by a peace that rushed through my core and visibly softened my outer appearance.

Almost instantly, my demeanor and countenance relaxed right before that janitor's eyes. We both observed something very real and very unexplainable happening to me. We both realized that though the man in the hallway certainly didn't know me well enough to cause this huge shift in my body, mind, and soul—there was another possibility: *God* was talking to me. Over the next few minutes, it was as if surging, silent waves of courage persuaded me that everything about my life was going to become new.

As this conviction took hold of me, I felt another equally strong impression. God was waiting for me to respond to Him!

How could I *not* respond to God's request to "Come," to take His invisible hand and turn my back on all the stuff that promised me something but had delivered nothing but heartache?

From the moment I heard God's voice, my life has never been the same. And no one has ever again had to convince me that God speaks or that He is real. I *know* God speaks. I *know* He's real.

Of course since that day I've learned so much more about God. Yet all the training or theology in the world has never made me love or trust Him more than the day I first heard God talk to me. He loved me when I was unlovely—who does that? He saved me and forgave me when I needed rescuing and forgiveness, and He came after me until I turned to Him. Everyone else had given up on me.

I've found that *nothing* will make you love or trust God *more* than when He tells you that He loves you just the way you are.

If you're struggling to survive, if you're feeling hopeless or desperate to make sense of your life, God has something specific to say to you. *I'm sure of it. Expect God to talk to you* in the midst of your "out-of-control" chaos. *Let God talk to you.* If you do, I promise your life will never be the same.

God Talks to Those Who Are Humbled by Their Circumstances

Over twenty-five years ago, I attended a conference in which five of the former presidents of a youth organization inspired their "troops" by telling us about God—not what He did, but what He said to them. They told us of their relationships with God, their conversations with God—how God talked to them, inspiring them afresh, even when they were greatly fatigued. They described turning-point moments when they chose to believe the impossible, identifying how and when God told them to move forward into unknown territories, convincing them He would go ahead of them.

Comparing my life to theirs at the time seemed futile. But the one area each professed as the most important possession of a leader was his or her willingness to let God talk to them, to give them powerful ideas at important moments. This was compelling to me because it was attainable by anyone. Hearing God speak, they said, was not dependent on gender or age, education or position.

God talks to those who are humble enough to listen to wise advice, willing to relinquish their plans for His, able to wait and not move ahead of Him impulsively.

This concept was revolutionary to me. More important, it took hold of me. Convinced, I immediately began to imitate the lives of these leaders by diligently spending time every day listening to God talk to me. Surprised, encouraged, and excited by my own conversational relationship with God, I wanted more. With very little effort, I uncovered numerous other historical, political, corporate, and religious leaders who spoke of a conversational relationship with God as a nonnegotiable component of their lives.

Peter Marshall, chaplain of the U.S. Senate in the 1940s, was one of those humble leaders who regularly and warmly spoke about his unique companionship with God. For example, he considered God's specific instructions for each day similar to a soldier who receives "marching orders from the Captain." As a spiritual leader to politicians, an exciting communicator to college students, and a preacher who spoke in filled-to-capacity auditoriums, Marshall's simple prayers and profound sermons instilled confidence in the average person by assuring him or her that God speaks—whether we listen to Him or not.

He consistently made a strong appeal to all men and women to humbly posture themselves, especially leaders, by setting aside time each day to listen to God talk. In fact, most of his recorded sermons included vivid instruction, first and foremost, detailing practical ways to communicate with God in two-way conversations.

Peter Marshall enthusiastically encouraged people to know God not by growing in intellectual knowledge, but by intimate familiarity with Him. Just as contemporary philosopher Dallas Willard contended decades later in his book *Hearing God*: "Spiritual people are not those who engage in certain spiritual practices; they are those who *draw their life from a conversational relationship with God*."[1]

When speaking of his role models, Peter Marshall always pointed to those who were personally acquainted with God from centuries earlier: George Müller of Bristol, Dr. George Washington Carver, Thomas à Kempis, to name a few. He referred to their letters, journals, and biographies. His mentors in the faith inspired him with their detailed, written records of how God dealt with them—when and where God talked to them, publicly professing what they believed God said when He talked to them.[2]

Peter Marshall encouraged not only leaders but everyone to talk to God about everything. "Just be honest with God," he challenged the collegians, congressmen, and members of his congregation to whom he spoke. "Just listen to God," he invited. His public prayers perfectly presented the way to God: "*We confess before Thee that our ears are often deaf to the whisper of Thy call, our eyes often blind to the signs of Thy guidance. Make us willing to be changed, even though it requires surgery of the soul and the therapy of discipline.*"[3]

God talks to those who humbly bring themselves before Him—young or old—to hear Him speak.

Why do we complicate what is so simple?

What do you lose by listening to the God who loves and lives today, who created man and moon and *who wants to talk to you*?

I encourage you to humble yourself before God. Open your ears and your heart to His voice. Listen. Wait. Tell Him you need Him. Ask Him to speak to you. Ask Him for courage and hope. Tell Him that you are struggling, that you are weak and afraid. Let Him talk to you!

God Talks to Those With a Simple, Childlike Trust

My friend and her granddaughter were talking about what to do when you feel afraid. The grandmother said, "Honey, if you ever feel afraid, just call on Jesus, and He'll come to you." The little girl looked at her grandmother, smiled brightly, and corrected her elder. She said, "Why would I have to call on Him, Gramma? He's always with me."

Is it really that simple? Can children feel or sense God's presence with them, even though He is invisible? Can a child hear God talk?

First Samuel—one of the Bible's Old Testament books, a historical account of the nation of Israel around 1000 BC—opens with the plight of Hannah, who was barren. During a tearful outpouring at the temple altar during the yearly religious celebration, she begged God to give her a child. *The Message*, a paraphrase of the Bible by Eugene Peterson, reveals her anguished appeal to God: "Crushed in soul . . . she made a vow: . . . By giving me a son, I'll give him . . . unreservedly to you" (1 Samuel 1:10–11). God answered her, and less than a year after her emotional altar encounter she conceived and delivered a son. In deep gratitude, she fulfilled her promise to God and dedicated her young boy to the Lord by offering him to temple service. She named him Samuel, which means, "I asked God for him" (1 Samuel 1:20 THE MESSAGE).

Not long after young Samuel began his temple service, he awoke from sleep in the middle of the night because he heard his name called out loud. He assumed it was the voice of Eli, the priest in charge of the temple, who resided in separate quarters. Because the voice was audible and so real, the boy got out of bed and approached Eli to ask why he had called out to him. Eli had not called for the boy and told him to go back to bed. But after Samuel came to him two more times, Eli realized this phenomenon could, in fact, be God talking to the child. So Eli instructed Samuel to go back to his room and listen carefully for the voice—telling him that God would talk to him.

This would be intense pressure on a young boy who was dedicated to temple service by his praying mother, don't you think? He was not an adult, a leader, a seasoned temple worker, or even the son of the head temple priest—he was just a child. In obedience, though, Samuel returned alone to his room, and upon hearing the voice again, he listened to God talk to him. The next morning, the child told Eli exactly what God had said, holding nothing back. It was a most serious message with disastrous consequences for Eli and his sons, who had been negligent in their priestly duties, even shaming God's name.

From that moment forward, God used Samuel continually to speak directly on His behalf to the nation of Israel, its leaders and followers, who very often seemed oblivious or rebellious to the voice of God.

But we should take notice that it was *as a child* that Samuel developed the ability to differentiate between God's voice and his own thoughts or the voices of others.

Hearing God talk is not dependent upon age or gender, education or perceived personal worth.

God talks to anyone—whether a child, a parent, people who lead, or people who follow. God talks to the faithful and the faith*less*. God talks to the helpless or hopeless. God speaks both gently and powerfully to those who are humble or are being humbled in front of Him and others. And God talks personally to those who are dependent on Him or desperate for Him, both young and old. God talks to those who deeply put their trust in

His name and His power and His Word. And God talks to those who are running from Him.

Must you be desperate or humble or childlike to hear God talk? Certainly this is not a prerequisite list, but a common list of conditions through which the majority of us hear God talk whether we are completely empty or completely full of ourselves.

Bottom line? God can and does talk to anyone. How He chooses to get our attention will vary from person to person.

Of course, how you and I respond when God talks to us can either complicate or clarify our lives, and it certainly deserves continued discussion.

CHAPTER 2

Why God Talks to You

Because I travel so frequently, I've come to expect the extra time and effort it takes to get re-dressed—belt, shoes, jacket—in any airport security lane. So you can imagine my delight when I arrived at my gate for a very early morning flight with plenty of time to spare.

Surveying the gate area, I perched myself about ten feet from the check-in counter—in a perfect position to board first. I was pleasantly surprised by the lack of hubbub that normally characterizes morning departures. In fact, the only people anywhere near me were two gate agents chatting it up behind the counter. Not even one customer was around to ask to change seats or sign up to fly standby.

Neatly organized in my "mobile office space" with phone in hand, purse slung over my shoulder, and roller bag at my side, I finally relaxed enough to get a little work done while waiting for boarding to be announced. I pulled the stylus out of my phone, made a few taps, and began watching the emails roll into my inbox.

Not a minute had passed when I heard a loud shuffle, then a huge sigh. I looked up to find a short woman who had positioned herself *almost on top of me.* She was wearing a casual jogging outfit and appeared to be both distraught and a bit disheveled. She didn't have the "look" of a frequent flyer, so I immediately assumed that her experience in the airport security lane had taken its toll on her—all the repacking, gathering, and patting down is often more than an occasional passenger is ready to handle so early in the day. But because she had nestled so close to me, *especially when there was ample space to sit or stand anywhere else,* I asked, in a CPR-ish kind of way, "Are you OK?"

"No," she didn't hesitate to reply.

For those of you who don't know me personally, I'm made for conversations like these. I love to talk to people, especially strangers!

So I asked a follow-up question: "What's wrong?"

"My father died yesterday, and I have to fly all the way from California to Newark, New Jersey, by myself. I don't think I can do it. And I don't want to be alone," she blurted out.

I dropped my phone into my purse, looked her straight in the eye, and asked, "What's your name?"

She replied, "Diane."

"Diane, you're not alone," I said firmly. I asked, "Do you believe in God?" I must have been using my "outside" voice, because in that moment, I saw one of the gate agents stop chatting and glance my way. But I pressed on when she nodded her head up and down, signaling a *yes.*

I said, "Diane, God will be with you on this plane. You're never alone." Then I asked, "Can I pray for you?"

She looked almost relieved and truly grateful . . . until I put my hand on her shoulder. She obviously wasn't anticipating that I would pray for her right then and there—in the boarding lane of our gate. But it was too late at that point. I closed my eyes to pray, but not before catching the glance of the second gate agent, who was probably wondering why a prayer meeting had just sprung up at his counter. So in my usual conversational manner, I began to pray for Diane—out loud. "Lord, be with Diane. Relieve her fears. You know how she's hurting. Please speak to her about her father, this trip, and her family. Be with her. Let her know that she's not alone. Thank you, Lord, for being with us during these times of sadness and pain. We love you. Amen."

I looked up and saw a genuine peace had come over Diane's face. She couldn't stop saying, "Thank you so much. Thank you so much. Thank you so much."

We boarded the plane shortly after our "boarding gate" prayer and didn't see each other again until a few hours later when she accidentally brushed my shoulder on her way back to the lavatory. I looked up just as she looked down; we were both surprised. She burst into a smile. Then she quickly bent down and whispered in my ear, "I'm not alone."

The first reason God talks to you is because He loves you.

God loves you so much that He is willing to reach into your heart with words of hope.

The death of a loved one, especially a parent, has the capacity to make time stand still like few other experiences.

My father, a typical midwestern blue-collar worker for most of his adult life, was a fun-loving, gentle man. Admirably, he was married fifty years to my mother and very content with very little. From childhood, though, he indulged in tobacco. His habit ranged from enjoying cigars with buddies on the golf course during his teens and twenties, to acquiring a variety of smoking pipes and stuffing them with aromatic tobacco that filled our home during the '50s and '60s. Eventually, he had to sneak a few puffs from his filter-less cigarettes whenever he could—outside, in the garage, or while walking the dog—thinking that he was hiding, or at least trying to hide, his habit from us.

For the last ten years of my father's life, he couldn't walk or breathe easily because he had smoked for so many years, and he just couldn't quit. We talked about his habit endlessly. Doctors repeatedly warned him of the devastation the tobacco smoke was having on his lungs. He continually promised us he would quit smoking. He just didn't—or couldn't.

Then one Sunday night in April, my mother called each of her three children, all of us born in Cleveland, Ohio, and now residents of sunny California. Mom asked us to come home on the next plane. She delivered the sad news that our father had suffered a very serious heart attack—and he was in a coma.

Over a twenty-four hour period, each of us arrived in Cleveland by order of our birth—my sister first, then my brother, then me. As if on cue, my father awoke from his coma within an hour of his youngest child's arrival. We held each other, prayed softly and often, realizing Dad had a very short memory. Showing pictures helped him get his bearings, but he often reverted back to an earlier time and place that was happiest for him. Nevertheless, we cherished every moment together, taking turns sleeping at the hospital.

For about five days Dad's breathing and memory slowly improved, so he was placed in a "step-down" unit and taken off life-support machines. Our family felt relieved that he would soon be coming home, and we started making plans for his recovery.

Comforted by Dad's prognosis, we all decided to sleep in our own beds for the first time since arriving in Cleveland, rather than camping out on one of the hospital couches in a nearby waiting room. So after the rest of the family went home for dinner, I stayed a few more hours to watch the Cleveland Indians baseball game with my dad. A die-hard Cleveland Indians fan that had not seen a World Championship pennant awarded since the 1950s, he had been energized by the Indians' exciting season the previous year. It had revived his hope for a victory that he had not felt for decades. Together, we thoroughly enjoyed watching all nine innings of the away game against the Toronto Blue Jays. And though it continued late into the evening, Dad stayed awake and alert through every pitch, every hit, and the eventual win. As the game ended, I asked Dad if I could say a little prayer with him—and as our hands met in an unexpected clasp, I asked God to take away any fear and send angels to surround him. I kissed his forehead, walked down the hospital corridor, and heard Dad ask the nurse, "Did you hear that nice prayer my daughter prayed for me?"

Our family awoke to a phone call early the next morning, asking us to come to the hospital quickly—Dad had experienced another severe heart attack. We threw on our coats and rushed to the hospital. As we entered the step-down unit, a nurse met us with the very sad news that Dad had died in his sleep and could not be resuscitated.

We left the hospital as quickly as we had arrived, a bit shaken, mostly stunned because we had no further opportunity to be with Dad or talk to him. As the day unfolded, we were required to make a number of decisions that would define my father's life. We made calls to our families, and many times we were so choked up with emotion, we couldn't even talk.

My husband, still in California, though he had gotten the news earlier in the day, called later in the afternoon to ask, "Have you heard God's voice today?" He added, "You don't want to miss God's voice." Then he encouraged me to spend time alone with God, talking to Him and listening to Him.

Our shared daily habit of listening to God talk has remained the same for years. Each day we open a 365-day Bible to "today's" reading—so listening to God talk to us on that April 27 would be no different. On that day, the New Testament reading relayed the story of Jesus talking about life after death, found in chapter 23 of Luke. The last verse of the day's reading said, "And Jesus

replied, 'I assure you, today you will be with me in paradise' "
(v. 43 NLT).

As if heaven came down into my heart, I heard God talk
to a daughter whose father had breathed his last breath and
who needed comfort and assurance. On the day my father died,
through my daily, planned Bible reading, I heard God saying to
me, "Today, your dad is with me in heaven."

Now, I don't want you to misunderstand me by assuming
that I believe this verse in Luke was written *about* me or *for*
me. But I do want you to understand that I believe God talks *to*
me on any given day by comforting me *through* Bible verses I'm
reading that day.

As I sat upon the bed in the very bedroom I had occupied
as a child, I both cried and laughed at the serendipitous communication I was having with God. Not someone who believes
in luck or chance, I rushed out of my bedroom to share the
verse in Luke with my mother and siblings. We determined to
prominently place this very verse on the pamphlet that we would
give to all those who attended the memorial service for my dad
a few days later.

Later that evening, the Cleveland Indians televised a second baseball game in their series with the Blue Jays, again from
Toronto's home stadium, which at the time was called the *Sky-
Dome*. Just as the game began, I was reminded of the sweet and
final experience I had with my father the previous night while
watching the game. Immediately—and at the time I didn't know
why—another thought came to mind. *Find the Sports section.*
So I did. I located the newspaper that had been delivered to the
front door of our family home every day for decades. I thumbed
through each section of the *Cleveland Plain Dealer* until I found
the front page of the Sports section.

In the mid-1990s, the Cleveland Indians' home games were
played in a newly built and newly named stadium, *Jacob's Field*.
At the time, their games were always sold out, and die-hard

Indians fans who couldn't get seats for Cleveland home games had loaded dozens of buses for the Toronto series. Fans by the hundreds were willing to travel for hours and cross the Canadian border to see their beloved Indians play in the *SkyDome*. The reporters were so impressed by the number of fans who had made the trek to Toronto, that they made it the lead story on the front page of the Sports section on April 27, 1996. Across the page in big, bold letters was the question *"Has the SkyDome become Jacob's Field?"*

Perhaps it is significant at this juncture to make a note that my father's name is *Jacob* Hunter. My grandfather's name is *Jacob*. And my only son's name is *Jacob*.

For me, the local newspaper's reference to *Jacob* and the sky was not simply a coincidence. It was a timely, direct, personal communication that came down from heaven into my hurting heart and our childhood home. I felt God talking to my family, comforting us with something we already knew but were grateful to be reminded of: On the day our earthly father passed away, he had gone to be with our Father in heaven.

God is determined to talk to you in ways that you will recognize—in order to spare you unnecessary pain and to remind you how intimately He is involved in every aspect of your life. God *wants* you to hear His personal, parental, protective, and powerful voice because He loves you deeply.

The second reason God talks to you is because He created you to communicate with Him as easily and as often as you communicate with others.

Most children raised in either Jewish or Christian homes have heard the stories of Joseph and Daniel, Moses and David, or Esther. In each case the main person hears God talk, or a messenger from God speaks to them on His behalf. God's instruction usually causes a crisis of belief, along with some incredible adventure that explodes, impacting many other lives in the process. The weary are strengthened. The frightened are emboldened. The powerless are encouraged. The weak are made strong. Closed doors are opened. The imprisoned are set free. Names and lives are changed forever.

As a toddler, my son, Jake, had a few favorite and very exciting Bible storybooks. Each night he begged us to read them over and over and over. Integral to each story was a very specific conversation between the person in the story and God. Interestingly, Jake never questioned how the individual heard God speak to him or if he even heard God talk out loud. He, like most children, inherently understood that talking is a basic method of communication. Jake didn't express doubt that God spoke in the past or in the present, or that God could be heard or understood by people of any age or of any occupation. Jake just seemed comfortable with the idea that God talked to everyone because everyone talks.

So on one occasion when I had to discipline my young son for unruly behavior, I sent him off to his bedroom for what we called a time-out. As he sauntered down the long hallway to his room, I suggested that he get "alone with God" and have a conversation with Him about his attitude. What is a mother to do when her child yells from his bedroom after only a few short minutes in confinement, "Mom, I talked to God and I told Him I'm sorry and He told me I can come out of my room now!"

If children find it so easy to believe that God talks to us and they possess a basic understanding of why God talks to us, then why does the idea of *God talking to us* seem so difficult for adults to grasp?

In his book *Hearing God*, Dallas Willard explains that if we could envision ourselves in a Bible story, then we'd view the Bible less as dogma and doctrine and more like our own reality. He writes that biblical men and women were no different than men and women of any generation, saying, "If we are really to understand the Bible record, we must enter into our study of it on the assumption that the experiences recorded there are basically of the same type as ours would have been if we had been there. Those who lived through those experiences felt very much as we would have if we had been in their place. Unless this comes home to us, the things that happened to the people in the Bible will remain unreal to us. We will not genuinely be able to believe the Bible or find its contents to be real, because it will have no experiential substance for us."[1]

Give it a try. Put yourself within the mix of the writers of the psalms as their friends or family members were mocking them or their employers were hunting them down to destroy them. Can you relate to their struggles? Do you have similar needs or concerns? As you read the following passages, do they inspire you to direct these words toward the living, loving God or to make them your own?

> Psalm 138, verse 3 says, "As soon as I pray, you answer me; you encourage me by giving me strength" (NLT).

> Psalm 25, verse 14 says, "The Lord confides in those who fear him; he makes his covenant known to them."

> Psalm 119:34, 38 says, "Give me understanding . . . reassure me of your promise" (NLT).

One hundred and fifty psalms contain the written conversations of those who knew God talked to them directly. This belief is evidenced by the way they poured out their hearts to Him, as if to say, "Talk to me!" Packed with verbal expressions of need, hope, and inquiry, the psalmists transparently and honestly relayed their utter dependence on a God they could not see but were convinced was always present and available to talk to them. Verse after verse of the psalms has the ability to carry you away to a place of passionate, emotional, two-way conversations with God. In fact, the entire Bible—both the Old and New Testaments—consistently reveals the pattern of God talking to men and women in order to make himself and His ways known to them.

Will you allow the living, loving God to talk to you?

- As the Creator over all, He has a *plan to reveal* to you.
- As the King of all, He has *power and authority to impart* to you.
- As your Savior, He is *able to rescue* you.

God talks to us because *He knows and we know* that talking is the best and sometimes the only way to deliver an important, even urgent message. Talking is how human beings reveal a secret or deliver confidential information. Talking is the oral method of communication that provides comfort to those who are anxious or afraid; it imparts wisdom or counsel; it can serve as a warning to save lives; and it can gently refocus or abruptly shake sense into someone!

The third reason God talks to you is because He has something significant to tell you that will help others.

When God talks to you, He invites you to cooperate with Him to either speak into the lives of others on His behalf or help them in their time of need.

Most of the great men and women of God whom I've personally known, or whose remarkable lives I've read about in books, had a common thread: they would tell you without hesitation that God talked to them. Frankly, to confess that God talks to you takes guts! But the written accounts of their lives reveal they specifically knew what God said to them, where they were when He said it, and more important, how (or if) they responded to Him. And very often they risked their lives or reputations because they believed God asked them to do something unusual or unexpected in order to stop or start something that they had no strength or ability to do on their own. They would tell you that when God talked to them, they rarely used their natural abilities but were required to believe beyond what they could see.

I could choose any number of people to highlight from the annals of history—those who heard God speak to them and did great things on His behalf: missionaries to China, such as Hudson Taylor or Marie Munson, who made the first and lasting inroads for Christianity into that nation; politicians who valiantly fought against injustice in the ilk of England's William Wilberforce; preachers like D. L. Moody, whose lack of education or personal charisma would never suggest the enormous and rousing responses his sermons elicited. Each believed—and more important, documented *and* modeled—that God personally talked to them.

Taylor, Munson, Wilberforce, and Moody realized that God talked to them because He had something to say that was either timely or life-changing *in that moment* for themselves *and for others*. And although God's instruction often sounded unusual, unique, or even costly to follow—they believed that what God intimately communicated with them was imperative and essential to the work they were doing. Each was dependent on God's words, not only to practically guide them, but to strengthen their souls like no other voice could.

But if I were to name one person whose life was uniquely defined by his ability to hear God speak and his subsequent willingness to cooperate with God in accomplishing impossible assignments continually set before him, it would be George Müller of Bristol, England.

Author A. T. Pierson details numerous stories—consistently extraordinary—about this ordinary but determined man who boldly asserted that he heard God talk to him. Packed into this 462-page biographical volume, *George Müller of Bristol*, are the dates and details of how significant funds were raised for his orphan work—when money was absolutely scarce—as well as practical insights into how he discerned that it was indeed God talking to him.

When someone leaves such a legacy, it is worth the time to extract from his life specific habits that might be duplicated.

George Müller's regular routine was to converse with God on his knees with the Word of God open, "providing a sacred channel of approach to God."[2] This pattern of using God's own words to fortify his requests only built greater confidence in Müller. He found great courage in agreeing with God, according to Bible promises and principles, rather than attempting to convince God to go along with his ideas, hopes, or plans. As God talked to Müller through Scripture, he in turn used the very same verses to talk to God. He became utterly convinced that God's boundless, fatherly love for orphans would be expressed through men in every possible way, and that through them their needs *would be* supplied. With each passing year, George Müller's conversations with God became bolder and more expectant. History records that he saved the lives of tens of thousands of orphaned children in his nation over a period of five difficult decades during the nineteenth century, giving all the credit to God for both the day-to-day and ongoing rescue work.

George Müller's biography is packed with the details of his entrepreneurial achievements and how instrumental he was in caring for more than one hundred thousand orphans in England during a time of disease, depression, and financial devastation, attributing the amazing success of his work to intimate discussions he had with God regarding every decision. When his work could have instantly been stopped for any number of reasons, he listened to God's direction and oftentimes overcame the impossible with faith and patience.

In addition to allowing God to talk to him through Scripture, Müller was convinced that God spoke through practical means and tangible circumstances. It was evident to him and others that *no amount of coincidence* could explain how *every specific need* of the orphan work was met with an *exact supply*, especially as George was adamant that he would not ask people—only God—to meet their needs. Though his faith and patience were often and severely tested over the decades, each time Müller heard God instruct him to buy more property, build additional orphan homes, recruit more staff, or take in more children, he trusted God to show him exactly how he was to accomplish this. It was said of Müller: "Without unduly counting the cost, he followed every leading of God."[3]

Müller's life suggests that it is neither religious training nor spiritual pedigree that gives someone the courage to stand against evil or oppression. Rather, it is that person's willingness to believe that God talks to them, asking for their cooperation to powerfully impact, change, speak into, or even save the lives of others.

Be assured, God spoke not only to the George Müllers of past centuries, but speaks to men and women today who will listen to His voice and *act on what they hear*! When God speaks through your life and my life, people see Jesus, they feel God's presence, and they open up to Him.

One of my fondest memories of God's using me to reach out to someone He loved who was searching and struggling occurred on a flight between my home in California and Kansas. I was flying off to speak for Fellowship of Christian Athletes, a high school and college ministry headquartered in Kansas City.

I sat down on an aisle seat in the back of a plane—one row from the lavatory—aboard a flight I was not originally scheduled to take. I was pleasantly surprised to be sitting next to a student who identified herself as a college athlete. I immediately thought our conversation would be fun. (A hoodie sweatshirt with school letters across her chest, very hip blue jeans, and a ponytail usually reveal the identity of a confident collegian.)

So I asked, within seconds of buckling my seat belt, "Where are you going?"

She surprised me with her red-rimmed eyes and quiet voice: "To see my ex-boyfriend."

"Why?" I asked.

" 'Cuz he wants to try to get back together," she replied, reservation in her voice.

I couldn't help myself. I powered through the next question even though we'd only known each other for sixty seconds—and I hadn't even asked her name yet: "Are you going to sleep with him?"

She didn't hesitate. "Probably."

I couldn't stop myself and asked her yet another question: "Why?"

"I don't know," she responded in a very despondent tone of voice.

I instantly knew why I was on that plane and in that seat. *I was God's messenger, an ambassador of the living, loving God.* I had a very similar story that I knew would resonate with her life. In fact, I had recently returned to working with students after years away, though I was resistant to the idea for all kinds of selfish reasons. But as I sat next to this scared young woman, I knew my words would penetrate right through her heart. I could speak honestly about my own painful and shameful experience as a student—looking for love by sleeping with men. I could tell her that I believed that this rendezvous was only going to steal her ability to experience true intimacy with God and others.

So I said, "I don't think that's a very good reason to go sleep with an ex-boyfriend. If you were my daughter, I would tell you to get off this plane and go back home."

She sighed. "My mother told me to go and have a good time."

At that very moment, I took on my full identity as a spiritual parent to this young woman. I began to share the humiliating details of my personal story with this beautiful college senior who was stuck in a middle seat and had nowhere to go for the next few hours. She listened intently, and we quickly became friends. It is not cliché to say this was a divine appointment. It simply was.

God was not on her radar before that plane ride. He existed, perhaps, but she had no idea that God wanted to be her Savior, or Father, or Friend. She certainly never considered God as someone who cared about her dating life. But she clearly understood me when I told her that "no man will ever fill the hole in your heart that only God can fill."

Before we deplaned, both going our separate ways, I asked if she would like to meet for breakfast at Denny's on the following Tuesday morning near her campus. She seemed very relieved that I would follow up with her.

The following Tuesday, and the Tuesday after that, we met to talk and pray. God used me strategically to speak to her on the plane and at Denny's, to invite her to enter into a relationship with Him, and to give her the confidence to be a young woman who didn't need to sleep with her ex-boyfriend (or boyfriend, for that matter) in pursuit of true and lasting love! I believe God reached down from heaven to speak to her through me. And because of our encounter, she and God, and she and I, have been friends ever since.

God talks to you and me by reaching down into our hearts with His love. God talks because He made us in His image; He created us to communicate with Him, just as easily and as often as we communicate with others. And God talks to you and me because He wants and needs us to strategically cooperate with Him by either speaking into others' lives or tangibly helping them in their time of need.

At this juncture, I encourage you to acknowledge that hearing God talk is only part of a conversational relationship with God. Those who take on their full identity and boldly do what God asks of them *after they hear God talk to them*—in spite of danger, embarrassment, or pending consequences—will be the ones who make the greatest impact, force the greatest change, or stand up against great injustice. They become God's "set apart" men and women.

~~~~~

CHAPTER 3

How God Talks to You

God intended for you to engage in two-way personal conversations with Him. He wants to talk with you frequently, and He wants you to freely talk with Him—even though you can't see Him. And just as you'd expect, the more you talk and listen to Him, the more familiar you'll become with His voice and the better you'll know Him.

The reverse is true as well. If you ignore God or deny Him, clutch stubbornly to a false idea about Him, or transfer an identity upon God that other people in your life possess—*any* of these behaviors can undermine, if not sabotage, your ability to hear God talk to you.

I encourage you at this juncture, especially if you struggle to hear God's voice, to try two short exercises before moving on.

First, read the conversations that each of the following men had with God: Noah (Genesis 6:8–7:5); Abraham (Genesis 12:1–4); Joshua (Joshua 1:1–9); and Jeremiah (Jeremiah 1). These are just a few Old Testament examples of how people from all walks of life and of differing ages heard God speak to them. As you read their accounts, reflect on how God approached them, how *they felt about* God when He talked to them, and exactly what they heard God say when He talked to them.

Second, stop to examine who God is to you—not who He is to your family or friends—but *who is He to you?* A. W. Tozer (1897–1963), in his classic book on the nature of God, challenged readers with: "What comes into our minds when we think about God is the most important thing about us."[1]

Who is God to you? Write down your thoughts in the back of this book or in a journal.

For example, when I think about who God is to me, not just one but many descriptions come to mind.

God is my heavenly Father, holy and awesome. Far beyond my understanding is the magnitude of who He is, and yet He is inexplicably present and always available to me, His child.

God is the Creator of all things, all-powerful and all-knowing, yet He is my Creator and empathetic with my humanity in all its weakness.

God is King over all mankind. He is royal and majestic, yet it's His love rather than His power that compels me to worship Him as my Lord.

God is the Holy Spirit, the wisest Counselor, whose instruction is always fair, always true, and pure in motive. Most significant, His advice is just and righteous, distinctive from the majority of voices clamoring to advise me.

God is Jesus the Savior, who died a sacrificial death on a cross—on my behalf. Jesus paid a price for my sins, which I could never pay. Because I have been so mercifully pardoned and undeservedly forgiven by His act of love, I cannot help but wholeheartedly follow and completely trust the One who died for me. Jesus lives forever and has promised to prepare a place for me in heaven with Him for eternity.

God is the eternal, three-in-one person, which makes Him infinitely more mysterious and wonderful than anyone I know.

God is mine and I am His.

Twentieth-century missionary and author Rosalind Rinker, in her revolutionary book *Prayer: Conversing With God,* wrote, "It is important for us to be able to think of our God as a Person, not an idea, or a principle, or even a spiritual concept. It must follow that whatever name we use for Him, that name must have some real meaning for us. There are literally hundreds of names for God in both the Old and New Testaments."[2]

It seems logical to assume that in order to hear God talk to you He must be personal to you. So let's explore this idea a little further.

Eugene Peterson, contemporary biblical scholar and author of *The Jesus Way*, writes, "God is nothing if not personal."[3] He continues, "By insisting that God is three-personed—Father, Son, and Holy Spirit; God-in-community—we are given an understanding of God that is emphatically personal. The only way he reveals himself or works among us is personal."[4]

If you consider Peterson's claim that the three-in-one God wants to talk to you *personally*, this will open up your capacity to hear God talk to you at different times and in different ways than you might have previously experienced. For example, if you embrace God as personal—*your* Father, *your* Savior, and *your* Counselor, the Holy Spirit—you can instantly:

Bring yourself before Him on bended knee in a secret place.

Invite Him to talk to you while hiking together in the woods.

Acknowledge that He is riding along with you in a car or airplane, or sitting in an office meeting or classroom with you.

When you consistently view God as *your* Father, *your* Savior, and *your* Comforter and Counselor—the Holy Spirit—you will begin to see Him as One who is always present in your daily life and who intimately knows you and unconditionally loves you. Your familiarity with Him and feelings toward God will naturally draw you nearer to Him. And as His presence becomes more tangible to you, you can quiet your soul at any time and in any place, admit your need, request His help, and invite God *into* you. In those very moments, you are perfectly positioned to hear God speak.

How does God talk *today*? Although this is certainly not an exhaustive list, here are *some* of the many ways:

God Talks Through His Written Word in the Bible

Andrew Murray, nineteenth-century South African religious leader and author of numerous (now classic) books on prayer, taught that the concept of hearing God speak was never meant to be a complicated, strictly intellectual endeavor, reserved for those who aspired to or held positions of spiritual leadership. He taught that *anyone* could hear God talk to them if they would read God's Word. He was adamant that reading the Bible was a necessary activity in the life of any man or woman who wanted to sustain a healthy, vibrant personal relationship with God.

Murray found Psalm 119 to be a perfect place to soak up God's words, to hear Him counsel, guide, convict, lift, and comfort the reader.

> Psalm 119:89 states, "Your word, O Lord, is eternal; it stands firm in the heavens." What doubts are demolished when you consider that God's Word was before all time?
>
> Psalm 119:114 professes, "Your word is my only hope" (CEV). On any given day, who does not need hope, guidance, or comfort?

Psalm 119:105 claims, "Your word is a lamp to my feet and a light for my path." Is there a day that goes by when you don't need important and timely advice before making a decision?

Psalm 119:160 explains, "The very essence of your words is truth" (NLT). Whose words but God's can be so fully trusted?

I encourage you to picture yourself having a personal, two-way conversation with God as you read through all one hundred and seventy-six verses of Psalm 119. To acknowledge that God is talking to you, underline or paraphrase any verses that relate to your life, encourage your faith, or motivate you to do something specific. Eventually, read each of the psalms as if it were your own personal profession of faith and written commitment of trust in God and His Word.

In Andrew Murray's book *The Inner Life*, I learned a simple concept that revolutionized my approach to daily Bible reading. He writes, "Prayer and the Word are inseparably linked together. Power in the use of either depends upon the presence of the other. . . . The Word gives me guidance for prayer, telling me what God will do for me. It gives me the power to pray, telling me how God would have me come. . . . And it gives me the answer to prayer, as it teaches what God will do for me. . . . Prayer seeks God; the Word reveals God. In prayer we rise to heaven to dwell with God; in the Word God comes to dwell with us."[5]

I've since memorized Murray's straightforward words as they've convinced me to let the Word of God speak to me daily, most predominantly and powerfully through my regular planned Bible reading. And after years of following this pattern, I echo Murray's words, convinced that God speaks most clearly and often to me as I read the Bible during my morning devotions. God's voice to me is as loud and clear as if He were standing in the kitchen conversing with me.

In fact, as I mentioned earlier, I use a 365-day version of the Bible that allows me to hear God's voice daily. (This resource has also helped me read through the entire Bible yearly.) And it never fails. *Daily* I hear God talk to me through the very verses I am reading—whether I am reading of a person's request for help in the midst of a battle or the heartfelt plea of a parent to help his or her family. The Word of God inevitably, through my daily Bible reading, gives me direction on how I might tackle a tough situation or comforts me by giving me hope in my anxiety. Over the years, I have consistently heard God's voice simply because I have been consistent enough to open the Bible to "today's" reading. Daily, while reading God's Word, I wait and listen for God to talk to me by impressing helpful or encouraging thoughts upon my heart and mind, which always address my present or pending concerns.

Even when you *aren't* sure it is God talking to you personally, you can confidently use His Word to reference, test, and confirm all things. (Second Timothy 3:16–17 says, "All Scripture is God-breathed and is useful for teaching, rebuking, correcting and training in righteousness, so that the man of God may be thoroughly equipped for every good work.")

God Talks to Me Through the Old Testament

For example, as I am writing this chapter, my daily Bible reading includes passages from the books of Daniel and 2 Peter. I didn't choose these verses and chapters as my reading for today—they were in place and prepared for me to read—but you can see how integral they are to my life as a teacher, author, and speaker on the topic of hearing God talk.

While reading through the book of Daniel, I am, first and foremost, impressed by the unwavering character of this Jewish boy who was exiled and put into the service of a foreign king. He passed every test and exceeded all expectations, leading his peers to live by higher standards than followed by those around them.

By the sixth chapter of Daniel, there had already been one attempt to execute Daniel's friends by throwing them into a fire because they refused to publicly deny God by bowing down to a golden statue. Incredibly, they survived, but not before professing their faith in the God they served—whether He saved them from the fire or not. Can I learn from this story or be challenged to live by higher standards in my culture because of how they lived their lives? Certainly. Is this story—their lives—relevant to me? Absolutely. Do I live in such an anti-God culture? Perhaps.

Because Daniel refused to stop praying to God, he was personally attacked by a gang of government leaders who devised a way to get him thrown into the lion's den (a common mode of execution at that time). One of the twists in this account includes the sorrow of the king, who deeply regretted that trickery was used to corner Daniel into this verdict and certain death. Yet according to the law of the land, the king had to follow through with the orders to cast Daniel—who would not bow down in worship to anyone but his God—into the lion's den. The king held out hope that Daniel might still be alive after a night in the den with lions and rushed to the site the next morning. When the king called down into the den looking for Daniel, he asked, "Daniel, servant of the living God! Was your God, whom you serve so faithfully, able to rescue you from the lions?" Daniel answered, "My God sent his angel to shut the lions' mouths so that they would not hurt me" (Daniel 6:20–22 NLT).

The king of Babylon at the time, Darius, was so impressed with Daniel's God that he sent a message to "the people of every race and nation and language throughout the world:

> "I decree that everyone throughout my kingdom should tremble with fear before the God of Daniel. For he is the living God, and he will endure forever. His kingdom will never be destroyed, and his rule will never end. He rescues and saves his people; he

performs miraculous signs and wonders in the heavens and on earth. He has rescued Daniel from the power of the lions."

Daniel 6:25–27 NLT

And that's just a little background information. Today, as I'm reading in the sixth chapter of Daniel, I ask myself, "What do I feel, think, or understand as I read these passages?" I'm inspired to believe in the God of the Bible who does miracles. And I'm reminded that God is with those who call on His name, who align themselves with Him, who follow His ways even when others—sometimes even a majority—do not.

So is this passage in Daniel *about* me or does it promise an outcome *for* me? Not necessarily. Does God talk *to* me *today* through this centuries-old written record of Daniel while I sit in my kitchen and read these historic words? Most certainly.

As I read the Bible today, I am reminded that God makes himself known to *others* through the way He works in the lives of His followers. My life, my decisions, my attitudes, and my words matter. On at least two occasions in the past few years, God has given me ideas and words that have saved a person's life—literally—just as the janitor on that fateful day saved mine. Both times a young woman came up to me after I shared my story and told me that she had intended to commit suicide later that day, but hearing my story gave her hope to hang on and the courage to tell somebody what she was about to do. Because she approached me, I was able to connect her with those who could keep her safe.

H. A. Ironside (1876–1951), an internationally recognized Bible teacher, author, and preacher, wrote in his commentary *I and II Timothy, Titus and Philemon:* "The Bible does not deal with one great subject only; neither does it speak to just one class of people. So as we study the Word, it is always important to ask, as we read: For whom was this written? What did God have in mind in giving it? Is it for me? Is it about me, or does it have to do with some other group of His people?"[6] These questions, if always kept in front of you while reading the Bible, will give you greater insights as you read. Ironside captures the essence of daily Bible reading by saying, "Now all Scripture is *for* me, but all Scripture is not *about* me."[7]

As I read the Bible on a daily basis, I never know how or if God will use something I have read to impact a friend or family member's life—so I remain alert. Numerous times I have been able to comfort a friend with a word from the Lord that came from my regular daily Bible reading. As a mother, I am always open to ways that God might be using Scripture to get my attention. For example, on January 1, 1997, after an intense New Year's Eve discussion with my college-age son about the dangers of underage drinking, we were struck by the timing of the day's assigned Proverbs reading: "My child, listen when your father corrects you. Don't neglect your mother's instruction" (Proverbs 1:8 NLT). When my husband, son, and I woke up that morning—after our intense family meeting—and read those words, we did not feel it was a coincidence. I especially felt God giving me a huge vote of confidence that He was right there with us, backing up and confirming the wise yet countercultural counsel of modern-day parents. On any given day, as I listen to God talk to *me* through the verses of my regular Bible reading, He gives me courage to be immovable in my convictions, to do the impossible, and, more important, to promptly do what He asks me to do then or in the future.

God Talks to Me Through the New Testament

As I continue with my personal pattern of hearing God talk to me through my daily Bible reading, I turn to the New Testament book of 2 Peter, chapter 3, verses 1–18. This is a letter written by the apostle Peter, exhorting first-century believers to remember what the prophets taught years earlier and what Jesus confirmed through His teaching while on earth. Within this section, He reminds them that:

> In the last days, scoffers will come, mocking the truth and following their own desires. . . .
>
> They deliberately forget that God made the heavens by the word of his command, and he brought the earth out from the water and surrounded it with water. . . . The heavens will pass away with a terrible noise, and the very elements themselves will disappear in fire, and the earth and everything on it will be found to deserve judgment. Since everything around us is going to be destroyed like this, what holy and godly lives you should live.

A few verses later Peter begs the readers of his letter:

> And so, dear friends, while you are waiting for these things to happen, make every effort to be found living peaceful lives that are pure and blameless in his sight.

What do I hear God say to me *today* through this reading? Initially I am reminded, just as Peter was reminding his dear friends, of the overarching theme of the Bible—the earth was created at God's command, by His word, and it will end at His command as well.

I also feel a strange comfort in knowing that thousands of years ago, and still today, there was, is, and will be opposition to God's Word.

Am I afraid and discouraged by Peter's warnings regarding the end of time? No, his words do not elicit fear in me. Rather, they bolster my faith, giving me a detailed account of how the world will end and eternity will begin. His passionate comments remind me of how I so often "live in the moment," and how quickly I forget about the enormity and certainty of what is to come in the future.

Is Peter's challenge *then* to live a holy and blameless life relevant to me *today*, a Christian woman, speaker, and author on topics such as prayer and purity? Do my choices of sobriety, fidelity, and a commitment to a daily devotional life honor God, even drawing others to want to know Him personally? Peter's timeless words fan the flame of my desire to live a holy and blameless life. They challenge me to live my twenty-first-century life based on God's Word—*whether or not* the Bible is considered politically correct or culturally popular by the masses.

Can you see why I consistently read the Bible daily? Not only did God talk to me on the day my father died, but on any given day I am exhorted, encouraged, enlightened, and empowered. But the main reason I keep coming back to read daily from the New and Old Testaments, Psalms, and Proverbs is because I don't want to miss God's voice. God talks. He does!

Martin Luther vividly portrays the Word of God in this way:

> The Bible is alive;
> It speaks to me.
> It has feet;
> It runs after me.
> It has hands;
> It lays hold of me.

Let God Talk to You Through the Old and New Testaments

Dear friend, let God talk to you *daily* through His written Word, the Bible. Let God's Word capture you. Let God take your breath away with His love and promises. Let God's Word give you hope for today and comfort for tomorrow. And if you don't initially feel encouraged or hopeful while reading the Bible, don't give up! Make it a point, before you begin reading, to simply ask God to talk to you through His Word. Then wait in expectation for some direction or inspiration, no matter how small, to be whispered into the ear of your heart and mind.

God Talks Through His Son, Jesus

Eugene Peterson, author of *The Message,* a paraphrase of the Bible, describes the writer of the New Testament book of 1 John as a pastor to those struggling to understand two of life's most difficult concepts—God and love. In the first of John's three letters, written after Jesus' crucifixion and resurrection, he begins by passionately explaining to them who Jesus was and is. In 1 John 1:1–4 (THE MESSAGE) he writes,

> From the very first day, we were there, taking it all in—we heard it with our own ears, saw it with our own eyes, verified it with our own hands. The Word of Life appeared right before our eyes; we saw it happen! And now we're telling you in most sober prose that what we witnessed was, incredibly, this: The infinite Life of God himself took shape before us. We saw it, we heard it, and now we're telling you so you can experience it along with us, this experience of communion with the Father and his Son, Jesus Christ. Our motive for writing is simply this: We want you to enjoy this, too. Your joy will double our joy!

John desperately wanted those who had never seen Jesus—firsthand—to know that Jesus was real and always present, that He can be seen and heard.

I can identify with John's words.

How Jesus Talks to Me

If you were to ask me, "How does Jesus talk to you?" I'd answer, "I see Jesus as much as I hear Jesus talk."

Before you get nervous, let me explain.

I'm forever grateful to my Junior Church Sunday school teacher—who had to be ninety-nine years old when I was three years old. In some tangible way, she weekly taught me and two dozen other little children that Jesus was "always present." A favorite lesson was about Jesus, the Good Shepherd, whose voice could be heard and understood by His sheep. She told us that it was His job to look for *even one* lost sheep and protect him or her, even at the risk of His own life. I often wonder if it was this childhood memory that helped me to know that God was reaching out to me, calling me when I was a young adult, far away from Him and on the brink of suicide.

Rebellious and disconnected from my family at the time, and barraged with self-destructive thoughts that accompany alcohol withdrawal, I recall hearing a voice that day, August 26, 1976, begging me not to take my life. Soon it became louder than the other thoughts that told me to commit suicide. If you asked me today, over three decades later, to identify the voice calling out to me that day, I would still say it was the voice of Jesus. Though not an audible sound, someone was calling me, asking me to come to Him, to turn to Him and run from everything else. The voice was familiar, strong, and appealing. I thought, *If I follow this voice, I'm going to find safety; I'm going to be saved.*

Most would call this a modern-day conversion experience. And it was. But I easily could have been the prodigal son who returned home to a loving father after ruining his life and wasting his inheritance (Luke 15:11–32). Or I could completely identify with the Samaritan woman at the well with whom Jesus openly, but not condemningly, talked about her immoral life. And though Jesus knew all about her escapades, he offered to exchange her adulterous life for His living water (John 4:4–42). *These were Bible stories I heard as a young child (and saw acted out on a flannel board) that explained the unfathomable love of God to those who didn't deserve it.*

I believe it was extremely helpful to have a picture of Jesus—the Good Shepherd—in my mind on that day in August, when I was about to commit suicide. I knew who was calling me to come to Him instead of taking my life. Deep inside I knew it was Jesus. I ran to the sound of His voice, and I've never been the same.

Over thirty-three years later, I still feel as if Jesus is standing, sitting, walking, or traveling right next to me. I'm familiar with the sound of His voice. Though not audible, it is consistent. I can sense when He nudges me, when He hugs me, and when He tells me that He loves me. And I respond to the nudge, hug, and suggestion just as I would respond to my husband's touch or request with a comment or a smile or a sigh.

I'm certain that the One who walks with me and talks to me is the same Jesus of Nazareth who lived on this earth, died on a cross, was buried in a tomb, and three days later rose from the grave, and later ascended into heaven. The same Jesus who was seen and heard by Romans and Jews and Gentiles, by shepherds and children and earthly rulers, who spent most of His life walking with, talking to, feeding, and healing young and old people, is the Jesus who talks to me.

I have a personal, conversational relationship with the same Jesus who hung out with fringe people, working-class people, and nonreligious people.

In fact, I picture myself "on the road" with Jesus visiting with all kinds of people in a variety of locations. I travel with Him and talk to others about Him. And He's always talking to me. I hear Him trying to get my attention in retail locations where I tend to lose my patience while standing in long lines, in the car when I'm driving a bit too fast, around my home when I'm tempted to procrastinate, in airports when I'm anxious, at the office when I'm concentrating—we're companions; we're together.

I like to think of myself as one of Jesus' disciples—someone who is very interested in what He has to say. In fact, I often hear Jesus talk to me through verses I've memorized—they're

His words recorded in the Gospels—Matthew, Mark, Luke, and John. For example, I love when Jesus whispers to me, reminding me *not* to let my heart be troubled and not to be afraid (John 14:27). He encourages me to keep asking Him for things, when others tell me to stop asking (Matthew 7:7–8), and He challenges me to believe that I will receive whatever I ask for in prayer (Matthew 21:22).

Jesus' voice, His ideas, and His counsel are uniquely different from any other. His voice is both thought-provoking *and* physically motivating—it moves me to be, to do, to go, and even to attempt the impossible for Him. I find that He doesn't ask me to meet the common standards but to exceed them. And I'm always encouraged by His voice—even when He corrects me. When Jesus talks to me, especially about my unfulfilled dreams, He fills my soul with hope, even if no one or nothing else gives me hope. And though Jesus' voice is patient, it is also relentless.

Hearing Jesus talk to me and seeing Him work in my life and the lives of others always makes me want to learn more from Him. I'm excited to be with Him every day. I just know if I had lived on this earth two thousand years ago, I'd be "on the team." I can see myself going with Him to pray for people or to heal the sick. In fact, those are the ways I most often hear Jesus talk to me. I hear Him encourage me, saying, "Go. Go and pray for that teenager. Don't just tell her family you'll pray for her. Get in your car, go to the hospital, lay your hands on her, and pray over her. Go in my power and don't be afraid to believe."

I also know He's talking *through* me while giving a lecture when I hear words come out of my mouth that I didn't plan to say. Words that weren't written on my speech outline just fly out of my mouth, such as, "At the end of this talk, I will be happy to pray with anyone who has a special need or prayer request or who needs to make a confession of sin." I've said those words a few times recently, and they've cost me no less than two and sometimes up to four full hours of nonstop, hands-on praying for hundreds of young men and women. Each time, I am certain that it is Jesus who prompted me to invite students to come up to a time of personal, one-on-one prayer, because I would not have given that excessive amount of time or energy on my own accord (after traveling all day and speaking on a platform for an hour). Yet with every prayer, I sense Jesus coming through me and over *each person*—almost replacing me—and laying His hands on them, offering forgiveness, healing their hearts with words He alone knew would be meaningful to them.

Let Jesus Talk to You

If you want to immediately experience Jesus talking to you, simply begin by reading from the first four books in the New Testament: Matthew, Mark, Luke, and John. Let Jesus talk to you through His own words. Underline or highlight any phrases or words that have significant meaning to you—perhaps they comfort or encourage you. Do they motivate or correct you? Place yourself in each story—is Jesus teaching a few people or many? Are you an attendee or an administrator? Are you a leader or follower? Are you attentive or distracted? Are you on the support team—praying, counseling, cooking, or preparing the way for Him?

How you hear Jesus talk to you while you are reading His words written in the Bible will resonate in similar and familiar ways when you're not reading the Bible. As you become more and more familiar with the New Testament gospels or the teaching found in the Lord's Prayer and the Sermon on the Mount, or the principles taught in each of the parables, the more often Jesus' words will become *your* thoughts, *your* mandates, and *your* strategies.

Let God powerfully and personally talk to you through the life and words of His Son, Jesus Christ, recorded in the four gospels and heard beyond those pages.

God Talks Through His Holy Spirit

Just before His last days on earth, Jesus began to instruct His disciples on how He would communicate with them after He left them and could no longer be visibly seen by them. As recorded in John 14:25–26, Jesus said,

> All this I have spoken while still with you. But the Counselor, the Holy Spirit, whom the Father will send in my name, will teach you all things and will remind you of everything I have said to you.

A short while later, while still speaking to the disciples (in John 16:7–15), Jesus continues to teach about the Holy Spirit, saying,

> But I tell you the truth: It is for your good that I am going away. Unless I go away, the Counselor will not come to you; but if I go, I will send him to you. When he comes, he will convict the world of guilt in regard to sin and righteousness and judgment: in regard to sin, because men do not believe in me; in regard to righteousness, because I am going to the Father, where you can see me no longer; and in regard to judgment, because the prince of this world now stands condemned. I have much more to say to you, more than you can now bear. But when he, the Spirit of truth, comes, he will guide you into all truth. He will not speak on his own; he will speak only what he hears, and he will tell you what is yet to come. He will bring glory to me by taking from what is mine and making it known to you. All that belongs to the Father is mine. That is why I said the Spirit will take from what is mine and make it known to you.

Just from these few passages, Jesus reveals an incredible amount of information about the person of the Holy Spirit: He is your Counselor, your Teacher, and the Truth-Teller. His voice will convict you of sin and guide you into truth. He will remind you of everything Jesus said while He was on earth. He was sent by Jesus, intentionally, to be with His followers. The Holy Spirit always and only brings glory to Jesus. It is His role and responsibility to make known to you what Jesus wants you to know.

Because I've talked to, coached, and prayed with so many people who live unfulfilled and defeated lives—always relapsing and never getting past their struggles—I feel that it is incredibly important to clearly present the power of God that is *available to you right now* in the person of the Holy Spirit.

The Holy Spirit is not an "it" or a thing. He is a person.

He is the holy person of God who indwells you, always revealing more and more of God to you. He illuminates the Word of God as you read it—almost lifting verses off the page to catch hold of your emotions and turn your heart toward Him. His words of counsel, comfort, conviction, and correction are designed to reveal truth versus lies, love versus selfishness, faith versus doubt, and right versus wrong to you. The Holy Spirit doesn't exist to make you happy—He exists to make God's love and power known to you.

And did I mention He is holy? This one-word description in His name and about His name—*holy*—defines the core of His message to you. He comes into you to set you apart for His purposes—to make you holy. The Holy Spirit talks to you—to teach and guide you in the holy ways of God.

If the Holy Spirit is to fully and completely reside within you, holiness will have to have its way with you.

How the Holy Spirit Talks to Me

How do I know that the Holy Spirit is talking to me and I'm not just hearing or thinking my own thoughts? *His voice is different than mine!*

> When the *Holy Spirit* talks to me, he cuts right through my impure motives and exposes them for what they are—greed,

jealousy, or lies. He gives me thoughts that are good and pure and true.

The *Holy Spirit* does not play favorites. He doesn't puff me, but neither does He tear me down. The Holy Spirit is very encouraging, very loving, and very affirming toward me. He doesn't condemn me or allow me to think or speak negative words to myself or others. He stops the "train of thoughts" that head down that track.

The *Holy Spirit* is far more generous than I would be. When I think "less," I hear Him say, "How about giving more?"

The *Holy Spirit's* voice never contradicts or denies God's written words found in the Bible; they reflect God's purity and power. I am reminded of faith-filled verses that cause me to agree with God's Word rather than ignore it.

The *Holy Spirit* does not tempt me. His voice leads me away from my temptations. He reminds me of the promises of purity and sobriety that I've made and kept for years. He fills me with an instant and powerful wave of courage to fight the good fight.

Sometimes the *Holy Spirit* catches my attention with a breeze— I physically *feel* the wind brush against my neck or cheeks or shoulders, and it's so soft and warm that I look up or around and am compelled to say, "It's YOU!" And I hear, "Yes, it is me. I love you."

The *Holy Spirit* is very patient. I'm just . . . not. So whenever I am tempted to lose my temper, or I feel anxiety creeping up on me, I know if I will get out of my own way, He'll fill me up with an ability to wait, or hesitate, to listen and not talk—if I just let Him calm me.

The *Holy Spirit's* voice, over time, becomes more and more clear and recognizable. In a variety or combination of ways, He willingly confirms His instructions, such as through serendipitous circumstances that line up either to open up or close an opportunity; or the affirmation of those who know me well, through the verses in my regular daily Bible reading, or through an internal peace that allows me to complete a transaction or make a decision without reservation. And until I'm sure of His will, He does not scold me for asking for clarification.

When the Holy Spirit speaks to me, I've learned to listen intentionally because I know that He *knows me* better than anyone else, and He can save me from getting hurt, even from hurting myself.

Have you ever gotten a traffic ticket? In California, we get issued a violation for "rolling" through a stop sign—not making a *complete* stop, usually in residential areas where there are pedestrians.

Twice a month, I travel the same shortcut through a neighborhood and roll through the final stop sign before arriving at my appointment. On one particular afternoon, upon making my usual "California roll," and before I had even turned the corner, a motorcycle cop was at my window.

His first question was "What does PRAAAAA mean?" My license plate was a gift from a former employee that she purchased thinking it would identify me in one word: PRAY. Only the word PRAY wasn't enough characters for a California license plate, so she spelled it out with five long AAAAA's. I'm sure you can imagine how pleasant an experience it is to tell a policeman who has pulled you over that your "word for the day" is PRAY. Needless to say, I got a $175 ticket and had to go to traffic school for eight hours. Not fun.

Two weeks later, oblivious to the fact that I had gotten a ticket for rolling through the same stop sign only fourteen days earlier, I was just about to do the same thing when I heard a loud voice say, "Look left." Of course, I didn't hear an audible voice, though my response to the thought was similar to someone asking me to turn my head—because I didn't hesitate, I just looked left! The voice did not say, "Hey, don't you think you should make a complete stop here since you got a ticket for rolling through this same stop sign two weeks ago?" I didn't hear, "Maybe the same policeman who was at this corner last time will be in the same spot this time." NO, there was no time for anything but "Look left." I instantly looked, and there he was. The very same motorcycle cop was waiting for . . . me. A surge of heat ran up my neck and through my cheeks. I was enormously embarrassed . . . and incredibly relieved. I had been spared! I had been given a reprieve. In one second I had heard the Holy Spirit get my attention and warn me.

What did I do next? I smiled and waved at Mr. Motorcycle Cop, made a complete and beautiful stop, and then turned the corner—ticket-free.

The Holy Spirit talks to me through thoughts that always help, always affirm, and always encourage me. Why? Because He loves me. He loves me. He loves *me*!

Let the Holy Spirit Talk to You

What might a conversation with the Holy Spirit sound, feel, or look like? Here are a few possibilities:

A silent battle wages within you—a tension between your desires and plans for your life and God's will for your life ensues. Either gently or relentlessly, the Holy Spirit will ask you to follow God's will. Will you go with Him or stay behind?

The Holy Spirit asks you to give *more* or *better* of yourself to an employer. You realize that ignoring His voice is as much an answer as making an extra effort. How, and perhaps more important, *when* will you respond?

The Holy Spirit reminds you of something you said you would do for someone else—and you've completely forgotten about it until the moment you hear His voice. You hear Him say, "Get the pen out, write the note (or write the check, wrap up the package, or buy the book), and send it *today*." Do you ignore or embrace the reminder?

You've been slowly or swiftly drifting away from spiritual disciplines that are designed to draw you nearer to God— attending church, reading your Bible, spending time in prayer, generously giving. You fondly remember how "sweet" it is to be near to God. You know this will cost you time. What, when, how will you return to God?

You feel ugly. Or you feel defeated. Suddenly you hear a faint whisper telling you how precious you are to God. It is a voice so soft and quiet that you have to really concentrate—tilting your ear toward the sound to be sure you capture every word. The Holy Spirit breathes into you the conviction that you are God's chosen. You are loved and special. You know you must hold on to these thoughts and not let them go. Do you take the time to converse with God in kneeling or written prayer?

You are tempted by an invitation or an image. You hear the Holy Spirit speak words—just as a loving parent or wise counselor would use, saying, "Stop! Don't go there. Say 'no' now. Don't give it another thought. Say the name of Jesus out loud. Tell 'it' to go away." Are you grateful or resentful for the help?

You've been wandering from solid moral convictions—not that others might know, but you know how you've been compromising. This comparison of your private self and your public self causes you to feel ashamed. You are at a turning point. The Holy Spirit shows you how you must change by giving you very specific (sometimes difficult), practical action steps that require an immediate response. Will you comply, surrender, or let go immediately? Or will you hesitate and waver in your obedience?

You encourage a stranger in some small way and then, almost immediately, hear the words: "Thank you for being my ambassador." The warmth you feel inside reminds you that you just joined God to bring needed encouragement to someone. Do you smile and acknowledge the encouragement of the Holy Spirit, or do you discount the encounter?

Under the power of the Holy Spirit, you find courage to shake off a compulsion that has been drawing you deeper under its control. Will you hate it and no longer give it room in your life? Will you tell others that you need help and accountability to stay on the right track? Or will you keep hiding it?

The Counselor, the Holy Spirit, reveals how your tongue or your thoughts have veered from God's Word—no amount of rationalization can defend them. Unkindness or prejudice is not tolerated by the Holy Spirit. He wants to obliterate such actions and attitudes from your life and vocabulary. Will you let Him work it out of you? Will you make amends? Will you relinquish old, immature behavior for godly character?

What did you think or feel when you read the previous examples of how the Holy Spirit might talk to you? Maybe you've thought that the Holy Spirit has never spoken to you. But perhaps the Holy Spirit has been talking directly to you through similar experiences and you just didn't realize it.

J. Oswald Sanders, in his book *Spiritual Leadership,* describes how vital it is to openly invite the Holy Spirit into your daily life. He simplifies what many consider a complicated theological issue by reminding us: "Each of us is as full of the Spirit as we really want to be."[8]

The Holy Spirit *wants* to talk to you!

Listen for His voice in the depths of your soul. Don't resist Him. Identify those words that resonate with the truths found in the Bible and hold on to them for dear life. The Holy Spirit's words will convict you, but not crush you. They will counsel you from a pure motive and comfort your soul for all the right reasons. When words such as these pass through your heart and mind, God is talking to you through His Holy Spirit.

Let the Holy Spirit talk to you.

God Talks Through Messengers

> During the third year of King Belshazzar's reign, I, Daniel, saw another vision, following the one that had already appeared to me. . . . As I, Daniel, was trying to understand the meaning of this vision, someone who looked like a man stood in front of me. And I heard a human voice calling out from the Ulai River, "Gabriel, tell this man the meaning of his vision." As Gabriel approached the place where I was standing, I became so terrified that I fell with my face to the ground. "Son of man," he said, "you must understand that the events you have seen in your vision relate to the time of the end." While he was speaking, I fainted and lay there with my face to the ground. But Gabriel roused me with a touch and helped me to my feet. Then he said, "I am here to tell you what will happen later in the time of wrath. What you have seen pertains to the very end of time."
>
> Daniel 8:1, 15–19 NLT

Whoa! How would you like to meet up with that messenger and hear that message?

Angels

There are numerous accounts in the Bible of angelic messengers who were sent to men and women—often *within* a vision—to deliver a message from God. Either the messenger interprets a dream for them, foretells the future, or gives them some urgent news to give others on God's behalf.

In the first chapter of Luke, Gabriel, the same angel sent to Daniel, visits both the priest Zechariah and his relative, young Mary. In this account of his angelic visitation (Luke 1:8–25),

Zechariah is on duty in the temple when Gabriel appears to him. He is initially startled and eventually silenced when Gabriel says:

> "Do not be afraid, Zechariah; your prayer has been heard. Your wife Elizabeth will bear you a son, and you are to give him the name John." . . .
>
> Zechariah asked the angel, "How can I be sure of this?". . .
>
> The angel answered, "I am Gabriel. I stand in the presence of God, and I have been sent to speak to you and to tell you this good news. And now you will be silent and not able to speak until the day this happens, because you did not believe my words, which will come true at their proper time" (vv. 13, 18–20).

A few things stand out: Gabriel is a very important angel who speaks to men and women on behalf of God at incredibly significant moments in the history of the world. He acknowledges that He is privileged to stand in the presence of God. He also expects to be taken seriously or there will be consequences—as Zechariah found out.

It is very interesting to me that not long after Gabriel appeared to Zechariah, he visited Mary, a young Jewish woman from the town of Nazareth (Luke 1:26–38), who was much more gracious in accepting that his words were from God. Gabriel greeted her by saying,

> "Do not be afraid, Mary, you have found favor with God. You will be with child and give birth to a son, and you are to give him the name Jesus. He will be great and will be called the Son of the Most High. The Lord God will give him the throne of his father David, and he will reign over the house of Jacob forever; his kingdom will never end."
>
> "How will this be," Mary asked the angel, "since I am a virgin?"

The angel answered, "The Holy Spirit will come upon you, and the power of the Most High will overshadow you. So the holy one to be born will be called the Son of God. Even Elizabeth your relative is going to have a child in her old age, and she who was said to be barren is in her sixth month. For nothing is impossible with God."

"I am the Lord's servant," Mary answered. "May it be to me as you have said." Then the angel left her (vv. 30–38).

These are only a few of the many biblical examples of angelic messengers sent to men and women when God wanted to urgently and supernaturally communicate with them.

Does God talk through angelic messengers today? Biblical scholars don't agree on an answer, and yet Hebrews 13:2 reminds us: "Don't forget to show hospitality to strangers, for some who have done this have entertained angels without realizing it!" (NLT).

Most important, if a message is truly from God—no matter who delivers it or how it is delivered—it will be proven true and reliable over time.

Prophets

Throughout the Bible, God also used prophets to speak to individuals and to nations. In the book of Haggai, God gave a message to the prophet Haggai that he was to deliver to two government officials in Judah. He was to instruct them to rebuild the house of the Lord and, most important, to assure them—along with the whole remnant of God's people—that the Lord would be with them. They received Haggai's message, and Haggai 1:14 records:

So the Lord sparked the enthusiasm of Zerubbabel son of Shealtiel, governor of Judah, and the enthusiasm of Jeshua son of Jehozadak, the high priest, and the enthusiasm of the whole remnant of God's people. They began to work on the house of their God, the Lord of Heaven's Armies. (NLT)

In the book of Zechariah, God's message was given to get the people to "listen up!" Zechariah (1:4) delivers the message from God:

> "Do not be like your forefathers, to whom the earlier prophets proclaimed: This is what the Lord Almighty says: 'Turn from your evil ways and your evil practices.' But they would not listen or pay attention to me, declares the Lord."

God talks to men and women in every generation through His messengers, sometimes just to restore their hearing. Most often He sends people with words to "fire them up," to send them out to do His work, or to get their lives back on track.

I am married to a modern-day messenger of God. He's a Christian counselor—and he's a wise man. I don't say that boastfully. I say that after watching his life impact and improve hundreds of people's marriages and pastors' ministries in the three decades I've known him. I say that because I am constantly approached by strangers who tell me how God "spoke through Roger" and he said just the right thing that saved their marriage, stopped them from making a mistake, or helped them overcome an addiction.

God speaks through Christian counselors who will give you biblical advice—words of truth—with such honesty that no one else has the guts to speak them to you. (Maybe that is why so few people want to visit with a counselor.)

God also often talks through our parents, spiritual leaders, bosses, or co-workers. They might make a very specific suggestion to you after you've asked for financial advice, or they might beg you not to do something that might jeopardize your reputation. In those critical conversations, pay attention. Is your heart thumping? Are your cheeks burning? Is the hair rising on your neck or arms? God will use His messengers to cause you to *feel* the urgency of His concern, to alert you, even warn you of pending danger. God talks to you through messengers so you *won't* move forward, backward, left, or right without His counsel, His voice.

God talks. He does! Listen for God to make His ways known to you through godly messengers.

How God's Messengers Speak to Me

In my personal experience, the messengers God has used to speak to me have most often been unsuspecting people placed perfectly in my life to bring a specific and timely word from Him.

Though it has been over thirty-three years, I am still amazed at the serendipitous encounter I had with a janitor who knew God and understood alcoholism, on the day I was about to commit suicide. When I entered a building looking for someone to talk to, he was the only person there. I believe he was standing at the bottom of the steps I had tearfully run down because God had assigned him to keep a divine appointment with me that afternoon.

Or how about the school secretary I ran into just a few months later while standing in the hallway of my old high school. She was a woman I had known as a student but I hadn't seen for years. She told me about a youth organization—one I had never heard of before—that worked with high school students in the area. Within a few months I went to work for Campus Life. Not only did they give me an opportunity to write my first book, but before the year was over, I had met and married my husband (who was my Campus Life boss).

I've had numerous encounters, often with complete strangers who I believe were messengers of God. I believe they were assigned to me by Him to get my attention at critical junctures in my life. They directed my steps, opened doors, spoke truth to me, or gave me an opportunity to fulfill a mission in my life for Him.

I firmly believe that God *regularly* uses messengers in our lives to give us time-sensitive, godly counsel that agrees with the written Word of God.

In fact, I often find myself in the messenger mode. I regularly look for a stranger to help, someone with whom to share the story of how God came into my life. I feel it is my life's purpose to find those who need God—especially those who are on the fringes of life for any variety of reasons. I am compelled to connect them to the God who loves and forgives them, just as that janitor so long ago did for me.

One of my favorite passages in the Bible challenges me to be God's messenger on any day, at any time. Second Corinthians 5:19–20 (NLT) reads:

> For God was in Christ, reconciling the world to himself, no longer counting people's sins against them. And he gave us this wonderful message of reconciliation. So we are Christ's ambassadors; God is making his appeal through us. We speak for Christ when we plead, "Come back to God!"

God desires YOU to be a messenger of His Word and love to others. He wants you to be an ambassador through whom He can talk and make himself known to those around you.

Devotional writer Oswald Chambers challenges me to see myself as God's messenger, writing, "God has moved you into His purpose through the Holy Spirit. He is using you now for His purposes throughout the world as He used His Son for the purpose of our salvation."[9]

Let God's Messengers Speak to You

One of the most powerful and immediate ways God will speak to you is through your pastor. The teaching and preaching of God's Word in your life should be considered as important and integral to your life as daily bread.

Invest in the preaching of God's Word by taking notes during each sermon. Bring a notebook, pen, and Bible to church. Later in the week, review the verses that were used during the message. Buy or borrow a book by an author your pastor quoted during the sermon and learn more about that person—their background, convictions, and theology. Each week, come prepared to hear God speak to you through whoever the messenger is on the platform.

Read, read, read as many spiritual growth books as you can each year—one a month or one a week. Read classic books on faith—by authors from centuries past, such as William Wilberforce, John Owen, or Charles Spurgeon. Read books on healing—so that you might learn how to pray for those who need God's healing—by authors who have spent many years studying the subject, such as Francis MacNutt or Neil Anderson. Read the biographies of missionaries or businesspersons, such as Hudson Taylor or Bill Bright, who left indisputable lasting legacies for God and whose lives will challenge you to do the same.

In fact, theologian Dietrich Bonhoeffer concludes that if a person is speaking on behalf of God, his words, his testimony, and his message will be coupled with indomitable courage. In his book *The Cost of Discipleship,* he writes, "Neither failure nor hostility can weaken the messenger's conviction that he has been sent by Jesus."[10]

God Talks Through Dreams and Visions, Acts of Nature, and Unusual Circumstances

Throughout the Bible, God used dreams and visions, acts of nature, and unusual circumstances to get the attention of people, to make an immediate impression upon them, to cause them to stop what they were doing and to listen to His voice.

Each of the books of Amos, Obadiah, and Nahum begin with the telling of a specific vision that each of these prophets received from the Lord—and each man was required to tell others what they heard God say to them.

A memorable example of how God spoke through dreams is found very early in the Old Testament. In Genesis 37, we learn about Joseph, who was his father Jacob's favorite son. Joseph received a dream in which he saw his brothers bowing down to him. Of course, this dream didn't go over well with his siblings, and they quickly found a way to sell him as a slave to traders traveling far away to Egypt.

Thinking they had rid themselves of their "dreamer" brother forever, their lives went on without him. Joseph, however, through a series of both prominent positions and unjust imprisonment in his new country, never lost his penchant for dreams. In fact, Joseph's ability to interpret dreams was the impetus for freeing him from prison and elevating him to leadership in the government of this foreign country (Genesis 41). Joseph's new position eventually resulted in the rescue of his entire family—a doting father and jealous brothers and all their wives and children—from a life-threatening famine. Remarkable!

In the New Testament book of Acts, Cornelius, a captain of the Italian Regiment, received a vision in which he was directed to send a few of his men to summon Peter in another town. He was even given the name of the man with whom Peter was staying. A devout and God-fearing man, though not a believer in Jesus, Cornelius complied with the instructions given in the vision and sent men to find Peter staying at a random home. They arrived immediately *after* Peter himself had fallen into and out of a trance. He too had been given a compelling vision that would define the Christian faith, differentiating it from other faiths. Within the same trance, he was also told that three men would come looking for him and he must go with them (Acts 10:1–23). So as all the circumstances converged—two visions connecting two strangers—Peter complied and went with men he'd never before met to meet a soldier he didn't know.

Very often in the Bible, God talks loudly and clearly through nature—through wind and fire, and even through a burning bush to His servant Moses (Exodus 3). In the dramatic account of the exodus of the Jews from Egypt, God used nature over and over to speak to both the Egyptians and the Israelites (Exodus 4–11). The sequence of catastrophic natural disasters that included plagues of boils, locusts, hail, and death were some of the most remarkable feats of nature ever recorded in history.

From cover to cover, the Bible describes one amazing written record after another of how God talks to men and women through unusual circumstances.

One such anomaly is the account of Gideon, who had very audacious conversations with God. When God asked Gideon to "save Israel out of Midian's hand" (Judges 6:14), Gideon balked. A bit fearful, and uncertain he had heard God correctly, Gideon asked God for a sign to confirm His orders. He left out a wool fleece overnight and asked God to leave dew on it but not on the ground around it. God did as he asked. Then, just to be certain, Gideon asked God to do the opposite. The next morning the fleece was dry but the ground was covered with dew. Not once but twice Gideon asked God for confirmation of his orders and twice God responded using a wool fleece. More unusual situations unfolded in Judges 6–8. Read them, and you'll be amazed at the way God talked to Gideon through unusual circumstances!

This and many, many more accounts of God talking through dreams and visions, acts of nature, and unusual circumstances are recorded in the Bible for every generation to read.

Having been a believer since 1976, I am convinced that God talks through the use of all of these methods *today* to communicate with you and me. I've seen the changed lives and heard the amazing personal stories of those who cannot explain how or why they were saved from an accident or how a random test caught a rare cancer early enough to remove it. Each is substantiated by an eyewitness, and the results of how God talked to them through a dream or vision or unusual circumstance are sustained by the evidence.

In fact, some of the greatest testimonies I've heard or read detail how God spoke in some undeniably supernatural way that directed a man or woman to become a missionary, to give untold sums of money to a needy stranger, to leave a lucrative job and donate much of his or her inheritance to God's work, or surrender their life to Christ even though they had been raised in another religion. In fact, my friend who has spent many months in India tells me that Muslims are coming to Christ through vivid dreams. He confirms that this is one of the clear moves of God in the "unreached" world today.

How God Talks to Me Through Dreams and Visions, Unusual Circumstances, or Acts of Nature

I mentioned earlier that I reluctantly agreed to go to Africa in the summer of 2008.

A young pastor from Penn State University kept asking me to join his small team and visit a specific area in Zambia where they had built a school for orphans. He had heard my story and felt it would truly resonate with thousands of parentless young boys and girls who were victims of AIDS and living in a dirt compound. I gave him a number of reasons why I couldn't go the first year, but by the second year, my reasons only sounded like excuses.

I finally threw out the condition that I couldn't go unless my husband, Roger, went with me, which I thought he'd be unable to do because of his heavy counseling load. To my surprise, Roger felt God indeed wanted both of us to go to Ndola, Zambia. He would give a marriage seminar to almost two hundred pastors and their wives over two days, and I would preach at the compound, sharing my testimony at a crusade on two evenings.

From the moment I left the United States, maybe even before I left, I was afraid that I was going to get malaria or die of something. For lack of a better description of myself, I am a chicken. I never heard of anyone who had a bad reaction to their shots required for international travel—except for me. And when I got to Zambia, I never felt comfortable or safe. I always felt afraid of something—the food, the water, or the gate guards with guns.

So on the first night of the crusade, our little team piled into our single vehicle and drove slowly for one mile (or it felt that long) down a bumpy dirt road to get to the compound. While the sun was still shining, our van pulled onto the dirt soccer field where a temporary stage and lights had been erected for the crusade. The sound of a youth choir practicing their worship songs reminded me of my favorite church in New York City—Times Square Church. I was OK at this point, *until* our one vehicle—our only transportation—was driven away.

My first thought was, *"Where is our driver going with the vehicle? How can we leave this place if something goes wrong? There are only six Americans in this compound, packed with thousands of children and a growing number of older teenagers who seem to be high on something and standing on the outskirts of our makeshift arena."* Fear struck my heart so quickly that I felt a panic attack coming on—and I don't think I ever had a panic attack before that day.

Not being able to control my emotions any longer, I *burst* into tears. (I laugh as I write this because it sounds so silly, but I was absolutely petrified, thinking we were in danger.) Almost in attack mode, I asked the young pastor where the driver was going. He assured me that he would be back before the service was over, but that did not console me.

I then turned to my husband, who seemed not to understand the depth of my fear. In fact, he firmly put both of his hands on my shoulders and said, "Snap out of it! Do you think Billy Graham cries at his crusades?" (Not funny then, but funny now.)

I took one deep breath, hoping my tears would subside, and they did, but only for a few short minutes.

It was dusk by then, and soon the sky would be pitch black. Out of the corner of my eye, I saw a fire in the field next to us. A fire! A *fire*? I was, once again, completely beside myself.

Standing near the tent where the choir was rehearsing was a group of pastors—men and women—who had attended my husband's marriage seminar earlier that day. I spotted one of the pastors, a large black woman, who was wearing her African clothes to the evening crusade rather than her church clothes. Something drew me to her.

I rushed up to Jenny. I didn't try to hide from this beloved pastor in this community the fact that I—the evening speaker— was a frightened wimp. I had lost all confidence in who I was and the message I was to bring. As a preacher, I knew this was a dreadful situation. You cannot speak to any group or bring any message in which you yourself do not believe.

The next thing I knew, I was completely wrapped up in her. (In America, I've never allowed myself to be so vulnerable with another person.) My arms were around her neck, my body flung over her voluptuous chest, her arms around my back. She began to boldly pray aloud for me. And I mean loudly. Anyone within fifty feet of us could hear her. She called on God; she stroked my head (another awkward moment) and let me wail. She comforted me as she spoke words of power over me. She held me—and I'm not exaggerating—for perhaps four to five full minutes. And she didn't let go until I had regained my courage, trusted God for our safety and the power to deliver a life-changing message, and was expectant that those who were seeking God would find Him.

As I look back on this unusual circumstance (it's not every day I cry like a baby in the arms of a complete stranger in the middle of a field in Ndola, Zambia), I'm grateful that God worked through Jenny to almost literally squeeze the fear out of me and breathe new life into me. Though it took quite a few (embarrassing) minutes, I finally felt reassured that I would be able to continue to do what He had asked me to do.

Over the next two nights, my husband tells me that more than one thousand young children and older teens came to Christ, prayed out loud with me, and raised their hands for healing. Jenny became my interpreter on the second night, and our tandem preaching will remain one of my fondest memories of all time. She seemed to know every word I said before I said it. And she delivered my testimony with the same passion that I do! She even crisscrossed the stage umpteen times "in step" with me!

I'm convinced that God reached out to me, enveloping me and calming me down through a strong African woman—in a way that I was unaccustomed to and previously too prideful to allow. But since that experience, even in the middle of a reserved or conservative crowd of students or adults, I'll fearlessly embrace someone who is completely out-of-control or overwhelmed by their fears with the same unusual full-body hug and powerful out-loud prayers. And their response is always similar to mine—a peace prevails that indicates to both of us that God is present, powerful, and in control.

I encourage you to let God talk to you in unorthodox, supernatural, out-of-the-box kinds of ways!

Whenever there is a possibility that God is talking to you through dreams and visions, unusual circumstances, or acts of nature . . .

First, test the instruction by how it aligns with the written Word of God. If it does not agree clearly with biblical principles, let it go (2 Timothy 3:16–17). (In general, it is difficult for the average person to discern between a spiritual dream or vision and a powerful subconscious desire. For most of us, dreams or visions from God will be rare. And yet, on occasion, God will use a supernatural experience such as a dream to direct our steps, answer a lingering question, or confirm a decision. I've known it to happen—but it has been very, very occasional. In every case, the Word of God always lined up with the dream or vision, unusual circumstance, or act of nature—it never was in conflict with or opposed to Scripture.)

Second, consult those in spiritual leadership over you—do they agree this might be a word from God for you? Proverbs 24:5–6 says, "A wise man has great power, and a man of knowledge increases strength; for waging war you need guidance, and for victory many advisers." Whenever possible, wait for enough time to pass to confirm that this advice, opportunity, or idea is from God. God is not usually in a rush—impulsivity is rarely His method of working. But on those occasions when God says, "GO NOW," you must be timely in your response. When there seems to be an urgency to the message, I encourage you to do these things with equal priority: (a) get alone with God for an unlimited amount of time and ask Him to confirm His direction to you convincingly, repeatedly, and especially through His written Word; (b) seek the counsel of those nearest to you, who know how God normally talks to you and/or works in your life. Ask them to pray to God on *your* behalf, asking for *His* counsel (not their ideas) to be revealed to all parties; and (c) then convene a meeting where all responses are brought together to be prayerfully evaluated.

Third, never consider a dream or vision, an act of nature, or an unusual circumstance to stand alone as God's final word to you. Allow it to confirm the message or direction you've received from God during your regular daily Bible reading and through the thoughts He has been impressing upon you through His Holy Spirit.

Oswald Chambers' litmus test for a dream, vision, or unusual circumstance is simple: "Never nourish an experience which has not God as its Source and faith in God as its result."[11] Your faith will grow as you develop your listening ear to the voice and thoughts of God. As you journal and share humbly with others about your experiences and encounters with Him, you will become more familiar with how God talks to you.

"I think God is talking to me."

Hearing God talk takes time and practice—which means you might not always be 100 percent sure that you've heard Him correctly.

Early in my relationship with God, my husband suggested that I not use the phrase *God told me,* because I could be wrong. (I tend to be impulsive and very enthusiastic.) Instead, Roger encouraged me to say, "I *think* or *feel* God is directing me" in a specific way.

Roger's wise and pastoral counsel has given me permission to express my initial impressions of how I hear God talk to me. This practice allows God to confirm His plans to me over time and through a variety of ways rather than relying on one moment or thought to be my single source of counsel. As I take time to hone in on God's voice, I don't struggle with lingering doubt or a fear that I will make a mistake or misrepresent God. Over the years, this practice has proven to increase my faith and improve my listening ear, giving me confidence to express to others what I "feel and think" God is prompting, encouraging, or asking me to do.

In Space and Time and History, God Talks!

God's voice is not magical or elusive.

In space and time and history, God talks in both audible and inaudible sounds, through unusual circumstances, dreams and visions, and His assigned messengers.

God talks to those who read His written Word found in the Bible. God talks to men and women through the warnings of Old Testament prophets, as well as through the recorded prayers of leaders like David (1 Chronicles 29:10–19) and mothers like Hannah (1 Samuel 1:10–11). God speaks—yesterday and today—through the New Testament letters, recorded miracles, and prophetic warnings, as well as through the revolutionary lives of Jesus Christ and His disciples.

God talks through the teachings of His only Son, Jesus of Nazareth. In the same words in which He spoke to His disciples, Jesus talks to you and me.

God talks to men and women—of the past and present—through His Holy Spirit. The holy person of God instructs, comforts, counsels, and convicts us by communicating to us through our intellect, thoughts, and feelings.

The living, loving God talks to men and women *today*.

Will you let God talk to you?

CHAPTER 4

What God Says
When He Talks

God has *so* much to tell you. He never intended for you to live your life without communicating with Him.

He will move heaven and earth to talk to you, knowing that what He says can change your life in an instant or heal your soul over time. *God talks to you in familiar ways with familiar words so that you'll recognize His voice.*

Because God is a fiercely loyal and deeply caring Father, He longs to tell you how much He loves you. And *because* He loves you, He will talk to you *throughout your entire life* with words that both convict and forgive, restoring you back to Him if you've lost your way. And God is not elusive. He wants you to know His will for your life, so He eagerly talks to you with words of confirmation.

The following is certainly not an all-inclusive list of what God says when He talks; it is simply a sample of the many ways God talks to you. As you read through these illustrations, keep in mind that in big or small decisions, God will guide your steps and make clear His direction for your life through words that align with biblical principles, circumstances that confirm His voice, and a deep peace that is assuring.

I share each of these stories so that you will not miss God's incredibly personal voice as He talks to you!

God Talks to You With Words of Love

Last fall I took an online college class. When I look back on the numerous books we were required to read and the dozens of papers we were asked to turn in during the semester, I remember one assignment more than any other. It focused on prisoners. More than just making me sad or angry, the sordid written accounts of abuse or injustice did their job—they motivated me to want to *do* something for prisoners right now, right where I live.

Well, I'd never visited a prison, and I simply didn't have any firsthand experience with those who were incarcerated. But the feelings of helplessness or inexperience didn't seem to stop the yearning to *do* something. Finally a thought popped into my head as I was writing a final paper for the class: *Becky, why don't you visit a juvenile detention center in your area?*

After praying about this idea, I didn't know how or where to begin such a process, so I zipped off a short email to a pastor at my church and asked, "Does our church ever visit the juvenile detention center in our county?"

He shot back a quick email reply, "We regularly take teams to the county detention center. Why, what's up?"

I shared my unexplainable desire to share my story with kids who were incarcerated and perhaps even pray with them, ideally during the upcoming Christmas holiday.

His next email response reminded me of how little I knew about prison protocol. First, not just anyone can visit people in jail. In addition, those who do visit prisoners must complete a thorough background check and receive official clearance—and this takes time. Next, any program must be reviewed and approved by the staff and chaplain of the detention center before permission is granted.

It was late November and time was short, but I felt an urgency to make something happen if at all possible. Knowing it was out of my hands, I asked my young and busy pastor if he would kindly ask the county detention center on my behalf. I committed to gathering a small team of family and friends (who could hopefully pass a government background check), if he could round up one of our finest church bands. Together, we agreed to bring a Christmas service to one of the county juvenile facilities *whenever* they would give us a date.

To our surprise, within just a few days we received approval from the chaplain, who had never heard of me or my story, to bring a special morning chapel service on the Sunday before Christmas. We were told there would be about seventy-five boy inmates and a dozen girls, whose average age was fifteen—and though there were many specific restrictions, we were officially invited.

About two weeks before the special day arrived, I began to contemplate what I was going to say to these young men and women who were incarcerated for up to twenty-four months for very serious offenses. Each time I sat down to write an outline for my talk, the many reasons this chapel service was probably *not* such a good idea would flood my mind:

> I didn't have any experience working with prisoners.
> I was a lot older than them.
> I was an emotional woman, not a strong, buff, or powerful man.
> I had never been incarcerated—how could I relate to them?

All the reasons in the world were still not enough to make me back out. Something was going to happen there—I just knew it. How did I know? For about two weeks, once or twice a day, whenever I thought about these boys and girls, I would instantly choke up and cry. I didn't even know them and yet I was filled with a deep love and compassion for them, much like a mother would feel for her daughter or son. I became convinced that God had something specific to say to these hurting teenagers.

The night before the chapel service, I sat down once again to try and write my talk. It was as if the time was finally right and I wrote out these words:

> *If you went to bed crying last night, angry at God, blaming Him for why you're here, He wanted me to tell you that He's not the reason for your pain or your problems. He's the answer. And He loves you.*

That was it. That was all I wrote.

The next morning, I took my little piece of paper along with family, friends, and band in tow, and we entered the prison. We waited quite a few minutes for over a hundred kids in chains and two dozen security guards to be situated before we could begin.

The four-man worship team—one of my church's finest bands—brought their very best playlist to this meeting. And they sang and played so loud you would have thought a thousand kids were in the room.

Then my pastor introduced me. I still felt stupid for being a mom-type person rather than a weight lifter–type speaker, yet shaking from head to toe, I headed to the front of the room with my little piece of paper, and through tears and a trembling voice, I said,

"God wanted me to give you a message:

> *If you went to bed crying last night, angry at God, blaming Him for why you're here, He wanted me to tell you that He's not the reason for your pain or your problems. He's the answer. And He loves you.*"

Then a gear switched. I took it to the next level and boldly powered through my story in less than twenty minutes to a completely quiet and captive audience. I ended with, "If you would like to ask Jesus Christ to come into your life today, to forgive you, to fill you with His Holy Spirit, please just raise your hand."

In that instant, I was horrified! I had completely forgotten that I was specifically instructed NOT to ask them to raise their hands—each of them was in chains and the guards didn't like movement.

Almost the moment the words left my lips, two-thirds of the boys and girls in the room raised their hands.

I looked at my dear pastor, my protective husband, a speechless chaplain, and the not-so-friendly guards. But in one unspoken moment of approval, our little team was given permission to approach each child whose hand was raised, kneel beside him, lay our hands on her, and pray with and for them, one by one.

We had been given only one hour for our entire program—yet at the end of sixty minutes, we had sung, delivered a message, and individually prayed for every boy and girl who had raised his or her hand.

As the young men and women departed the room—in groups of six inmates and one guard—I was allowed to shake each hand and say good-bye. The youngest and smallest boy of the entire group, perhaps only fourteen years old, looked me straight in the eye and said, "That was me."

I said, "Pardon me?" I didn't understand what he meant.

He repeated himself. "That was me. I am the one who went to bed crying last night. I told God I hated Him for putting me here. That message was from God to me."

That young inmate heard God talk to him, telling him personally that—no matter what he'd done, where he'd been, or what he'd said—He loved him. That boy had no idea that God loved him with "Ahavah" love (Hebrew)—passionate, possessive, permanent, and costly love. God's love simply transcended his pain and swept into his heart with words he could understand.

Romans 8:35, 38–39 says,

> Can anything ever separate us from Christ's love? Does it mean he no longer loves us if we have trouble or calamity, or are persecuted, or hungry, or destitute, or in danger, or threatened with death? . . . And I am convinced that nothing can ever separate us from God's love. Neither death nor life, neither angels nor demons, neither our fears for today nor our worries about tomorrow—not even the powers of hell can separate us from God's love. No power in the sky above or in the earth below—indeed, nothing in all creation will ever be able to separate us from the love of God that is revealed in Christ Jesus our Lord. (NLT)

God loves you. *If you've never read a Bible or know what it says, even if you've been stubborn or disobedient or resistant to His voice,* God will talk to you through any means necessary to express His undying love toward you. Psalm 139:16 says, "You saw me before I was born. Every day of my life was recorded in your book. Every moment was laid out before a single day had passed" (NLT).

God will do whatever it takes to get your attention so that you'll know-like-you-know that He indeed is talking to you.

God Talks to You With Words of Conviction

When God "calls you out," you can't help but come forward.

During my travels to twenty-three college campuses over forty days in 2006, I began to realize that many young men—especially those in leadership—were heavily involved in pornography. This was not a hunch. This was what they were telling me.

After about fifteen campus visits, I felt as if I had uncovered something sinister. I honestly thought, "Can I be the only one hearing these confessions of addiction to pornography by men in worship bands or on ministry teams or on leadership councils? What is going on?"

So in a random, unplanned moment in the middle of my talk to over one thousand collegians on a large northwestern university campus, I blurted out, "Frankly, I think there is a spirit of pornography over the young men of this generation."

That was a loaded statement for a number of reasons! First of all, it sounds a little melodramatic. Second, it's accusatory. Third, it's controversial in a coed crowd. And finally, it's rarely a subject that is openly discussed.

But the words just tumbled out of my mouth.

Less than a minute after that most awkward moment, a very personable young man, a senior campus ministry leader who had emceed the evening, was standing next to me. Through my peripheral vision I had seen him walking *up to* the stage, but I never thought I'd see him *on* the stage, right beside me, until I had finished my talk.

He asked, "Can I say something?"

I'm thinking, *Are you kidding me? Now is not the time for an announcement!* With over a thousand pairs of eyes watching to see how I'd react to this very unusual interruption, I asked in a whisper, "Right now?"

He nodded his head. I had one second to decide what to do and, throwing all caution to the wind, handed him the mic.

Unprompted by anyone—including me—he proceeded to confess his addiction to pornography (since elementary school) to the entire audience. We were all speechless.

This young man, I later found out, was getting married in the summer and entering seminary in the fall. He had everything to lose by coming forward—his reputation would be marred and his integrity would be questioned for a long time to follow. Somehow, in that hour, God powerfully both exposed and demolished the stronghold of a sin that he'd held on to for ten long years.

Why did he come forward? He appeared to have much more to gain by keeping his mouth shut than by coming forward.

He heard God talk to him.

He proceeded to invite anyone in the audience to meet with him the next evening in his dorm lobby to "deal" with pornography.

Then he stopped talking, and we looked at each other.

It was obvious that my message was over, but God's message was just beginning. Dozens of young men in the audience streamed out of their seats and came forward to kneel and pray and to be prayed over by their campus pastors.

Who does this? Who openly declares to their peers that he or she is struggling with a secret sin?

One who is convicted of sin by the living, loving God will have those "white lightning" moments, when he or she sees a sin for the first time as poisonous, deadly, and self-destructive—as if his or her blind eyes have been miraculously opened. They will come forward publicly, in humiliation. In that moment they no longer care what people think of them or their sin. They just want OUT. They want to come clean, feel clean, and be clean.

God talks to you and me with words that convict us of specific sins so that *we'll be set free* from the lies, shame, and guilt that are attached to them. He wants us to be liberated from the habits that strangle us and sever our personal relationships with Him and with others.

Life Together, Dietrich Bonhoeffer's classic book exploring faith within a community, contains the simplest explanation of how to let God heal and restore you after He has convicted you of sin. Bonhoeffer considers the moments *after* conviction incredibly strategic—where "breakthrough-to-new-life occurs."[1] He suggests taking immediate action in those moments when you sense, hear, know, and feel God convicting you *by publicly confessing your wrongs* to another human being. He writes, "In the confession of concrete sins the old man dies a painful, shameful death before the eyes of a brother. . . . In the deep mental and physical pain of humiliation before a brother—which means, before God—we experience the Cross of Jesus as our rescue and salvation. The old man dies, but it is God who has conquered him."[2]

By the way, God will talk to you and me with words that convict us on a regular basis, if we will let Him!

Just this week, I was given a thought that exposed a prideful, judgmental attitude I was harboring. Interestingly, I had somehow not felt the sting of conviction over the past few months, though I should have, until I read something as part of a group assignment.

It was an instant series of thoughts that caught my attention and convicted me. I was planning to read the entire chapter of Luke 17. As I got to verses 3–4: "So watch yourselves! If another believer sins, rebuke that person; then if there is repentance, forgive. Even if that person wrongs you seven times a day and each time turns again and asks forgiveness, you must forgive" (NLT), the following thought entered my mind: *You have not really forgiven that pastor at the neighboring church who had an affair this summer and has since returned to his wife and ministry. You're smug and judgmental. And you've even let your distrust of him be known to someone else.* Then I could almost hear and see myself giving my spiel at a seminar, saying, "Forgiveness is not an option for a believer." Obviously, I've read this verse many times before, but when I read it that morning, God talked to me with words of conviction. His words prompted me to take personal action.

When God talks to you with words of conviction, He intends to correct you, not crush you. How quickly you respond when you hear His words of conviction will change your life and very possibly change or save the lives of others by the way you respond.

God Talks to You With Words of Forgiveness

Earlier this week, I received an email from someone I met recently.

When I delivered a second chapel presentation on her campus, Kelly[3] was the last of nearly one hundred students who waited afterward for prayer. By this time I was running late. I should have been on the road for another meeting over an hour earlier! But just as I was about to walk away from my assigned "last student" and pack up to travel south, Kelly added herself to the line. I turned to her and said politely, "I really can't stay any longer," but there was so much distress on her face, I stopped and took a deep breath before saying or doing anything more. In that moment, I felt like two strong hands were pressing down on my shoulders—holding my feet stationary.

Over the next ten minutes, this eighteen-year-old young woman physically shook as she told her story of a broken home life, drinking and sexual experimentation at a very early age, a rape, and an addiction to alcohol that was obsessively controlling her. Humiliated and afraid as she was to tell anyone, especially on her campus, she had hoped I could at least understand her shame.

Understand? I couldn't hold back my tears. I put my two hands on her shoulders and prayed for many things, but especially for God to give her peace, to forgive her, and somehow to show her how much He loved her. We determined to stay in touch and met three or four times over the next few months. Each time we talked and prayed I knew we were in a fierce battle, not only for her sobriety, but for the restoration of her soul.

The last time I saw her was only a few weeks ago. She had gotten a ride from campus to meet me at my church. We sat together and got caught up before the sermon started. She had been drinking, and in her life, as it had in mine, alcohol usually led to other trouble.

Unbeknownst to either of us, the message was based on the passage in Ephesians 5:18: "Do not get drunk on wine. . . . Instead, be filled with the Spirit." She smiled when I shamelessly winked at her and poked her ribs. God was not going to let her go.

After the sermon, we knelt together, and she prayed out loud, tearfully asking God to forgive her once again. During her prayer, we both knew the stranglehold had finally been broken. She was done. The anxious back-and-forth battle was over. She resolved to leave the party girl behind—and the friends that went along with that old girl. She would pursue new friends, a new identity, and the freedom from addiction that comes with that new life.

So this week, when I received the following email from her (used with permission and unedited), I couldn't help but think of how God talks to us with words of forgiveness, intended *not only for us* but to restore the souls of others, as well.

> Last night my roommate and I are sitting in our room doing homework and this girl down the hall comes in and asks if she can talk to me for a minute. I got up and followed her to her room, and as soon as I shut the door behind me she just started crying. She didn't even say anything for the first few minutes, she just cried. I sat with her and held her while she cried. She told me that the previous night she went to a party there and got drunk and almost lost her virginity to some guy. This girl had never kissed a boy before, she had never been drunk before, she went [to] a Christian school since kindergarten. She's a good girl. She told me she would have never done that much with him if she hadn't been drinking. She went on and on about how this isn't who she is, she's not this kind of person. I can't remember the last time I've seen somebody cry this much.
>
> She hadn't told anyone what had happened. She was angry, sad, disappointed, and broken. She knew my past and had seen the change in my life and she said she needed to tell somebody so bad and that I was the only person she knew who would understand. And I did. I knew exactly how she felt. I knew every single name she had for herself. I know what it feels like

to wake up the next morning and hate yourself. Five minutes into our conversation she asked if I would pray for her. I said of course and I laid my hands on her and I prayed. She was crying the entire time and my eyes were watering as I prayed out loud for her. She told me she didn't know if she could ever forgive herself and I just shared with her everything I know so far, and it wasn't anything she hasn't heard before but I think it was different because she was desperate. I reminded her of God's grace and forgiveness and love. I read her the verses you gave me and told me to memorize: 2 Corinthians 5:17–20; 1 John 1:9; James 5:16.

And I'm sure she's heard them before but she just soaked each verse in, I think because she needed them now more than ever. I suggested that she pray and tell God what happened, to receive forgiveness, and comfort, and to begin the healing process. She said that she has felt so distant from God lately. That she knows He's there but she doesn't feel Him. She told me how badly she wants to feel Him and feel His presence, how badly she wants to believe that He's there. I told her to tell God exactly what she just told me. So she prayed. For a good amount of time she just laid everything down before the Lord. She confessed all of the sin and told Him how desperate she was for Him.

It was amazing.

Not so long ago, it was me who was crying, broken and ashamed. Now I'm the one catching tears.

That whole thing took a couple of hours and when I got back to my room it was past midnight and I just got on my knees and thanked the Lord. I was so humbled by what had happened, by what I got to witness and experience.

Her letter speaks to me. It should speak to every parent, every student, every pastor, every administrator, every friend, every roommate, every spouse, and every teacher.

This young generation desperately needs to be restored to spiritual, physical, and emotional wholeness. Many have been abandoned. Many have made destructive personal mistakes or have been horribly abused. Many feel as if they are being ignored, judged, or left to fend for themselves. They, like every generation, are desperate for forgiveness and restoration.

God is trying to reach every young man and woman through anyone who will be a spiritual parent to them and offer these simple words: "God loves you just the way you are. He forgives you."

Paul, in Galatians 6:1, writes, "Brothers, if someone is caught in a sin, you who are spiritual should restore him gently."

If God has restored your soul, if He has brought you back to himself, take on this identity and speak God's words of restoration into the lives of those He puts into your life. Pray David's words, saying,

> Create in me a pure heart, O God, and renew a steadfast spirit within me. Do not cast me from your presence or take your Holy Spirit from me. Restore to me the joy of your salvation and grant me a willing spirit, to sustain me. Then I will teach transgressors your ways, and sinners will turn back to you.
>
> Psalm 51:10–13

God Talks to You With Words of Confirmation

I rarely tell this story, mostly because it is so uncanny. But anyone who is dating, single, or engaged *loves* to hear me share the unusual way that God confirmed to me and Roger that we were to get married. (There were many other words of confirmation to us, but this one was the most exciting and fun.)

A little background is necessary.

Roger was my boss at Cleveland Campus Life/Youth for Christ. He was thirty and I was twenty-two. I was newly sober, a newly trained youth worker, and because I had such an openly conversational relationship with God, I was always asking God to talk to me or show me what I should do next. I was often accused by more "mature" Christians of being too childlike in my faith, possibly even exhausting God by talking to Him about too many things—everything, anything, even insignificant things. But Roger actually seemed to like this about me! In fact, he often said that he "kept me around" because of my faith.

By November 1977, it was becoming evident that my relationship with Roger was changing from co-worker into something more. We had never kissed or even dated, but we had spent almost every day together during the previous year working side by side in the office or heading up club meetings, staff meetings, and retreats for the students in our city.

A turning point in our relationship occurred while at the annual Campus Life Weekend in November. While playing in the Mud Bowl, a rowdy coed football game between staff and students, Roger, while attempting to tackle me, fell and broke his glasses.

On that Sunday night, after dropping off all the kids after camp, we sat in his van and talked about our relationship in a very serious, though cryptic, manner. He said, "I don't want to ruin our ministry relationship by dating. We need to pray and ask God to confirm our relationship, to ask Him for a Scripture." So we did.

As a relatively new and impressionable young Christian, I thought, "Is this how Christians do the dating/marriage thing?" Though Roger's idea for confirming our relationship was foreign to my previous, non-Christian way of serious dating, I was very open and excited to do just what he suggested. (From the day I became a Christian, I have always expected God to do something or say something unpredictable, and He has. Even though this was a strange request, it was not out of character for me to think that God would *certainly* give us a Scripture.)

The next morning, Roger did what any man who needed new eyeglasses would do. He asked me—the girl who might be spending a lot more time with him in the future—to go shopping with him to pick out new frames.

He picked me up at my college dorm (where I was living for the semester), and we drove together to an eyeglass store in our small college town of Berea, Ohio. The eyeglasses that I liked and the ones he liked were not the same (some things never change!). So we decided to check out the frames at another eyeglass store. Before leaving the first store, I wanted to be sure that we could relocate the "cool" frames I liked (which he considered "too far out"), just in case we were unable to find glasses we both liked at the next store. In order to do that, I looked for an inscription on the inside earpiece of the frame, near the temple. Inscribed on the frame was this: COL 3.

I said, "Roger, look! Maybe God is giving us a verse—Colossians 3!?" Granted, it had been less than twenty-four hours, we weren't studying in our Bibles or sitting in church, but hey, it was a reference to a Bible verse. I began to rifle through my purse, but my trusty pocket Bible was not there. How strange. I was really excited to see what verses were located in Colossians 3, but without a Bible, I wasn't going to find out until later that day.

We left the store, got in the van, traveled only three blocks, and walked into the only other eyeglass store in town. The older gentleman who had owned that establishment for decades warmly greeted us. To this day I remember his face and his name—Mr. Farkas. But more significant, I remember what he said and did that impacted Roger's and my life. He said, "Hello. Thanks for coming in today. I am a Gideon. Do you mind if I give you EACH a little pocket Bible?" (The Gideons—an association of Christian businesspersons—have distributed millions of Bibles to hospitals, hotels, and individuals since 1899.)

Did I mind? I snatched that little 3" x 4" emerald green Revised Berkeley Version Bible (1976 edition) from his hand with the untamed enthusiasm of a woman who is about to receive a marriage proposal! Roger, always more patient than me, allowed the store owner to methodically show us dozens of eyeglass frames. THEN we ran to the car and opened our Bibles. Not knowing what we would find in the third chapter of Colossians, I read out loud the first verse I turned to:

Therefore as God's chosen, set apart and enjoying His love; clothe yourself with tenderness of heart, kindliness, humility, gentleness, patient endurance (v. 12).

Roger read aloud these verses to me:

Wives, be submissive to your husbands, as it is becoming in the Lord to do. Husbands, love your wives (vv. 18–19).

A little embarrassed, we burst into laughter. Then suddenly we felt the seriousness of the moment. We had asked God for a Scripture confirmation—was this just a huge coincidence? Roger was skeptical—or maybe he was just a little weak in the knees. He expressed concern that this whole conversation was moving too fast. I, on the other hand, was thrilled!

That night, alone in his apartment, Roger told God of his concern. Then he turned to his favorite daily devotional, *My Utmost for His Highest*, written by Oswald Chambers. It read:

"All things work together for good to them that love God" (Romans 8:28). The circumstances of a saint's life are ordained of God. In the life of a saint there is no such thing as chance. God by His providence brings you into circumstances that you cannot understand at all, but the Spirit of God understands. . . . Never put your hand in front of the circumstances and say—I am going to be my own providence here, I must watch this and guard that. All your circumstances are in the hand of God; therefore never think it is strange concerning the circumstances you are in.[4]

This was only one of the numerous confirmations, including private and prayerful counsel from Roger's pastor, that prompted Roger only a few days later to ask my dad first, then me, if he could marry me. We said, "Yes!" And Roger and I have been married over thirty-one years.

In January 1978, about a month before we were married, Roger was shaving, and while looking in the mirror, it struck him: he didn't buy the glasses from the first eyeglass store. He had purchased a pair of frames from Mr. Farkas. With a bit of apprehension, he looked inside his frames, on the earpiece near the temple. This pair of glasses had its own unique inscription: one word was placed within a five-cornered star: *YES!*

We have a little box of mementos that we've saved over the years. Included in its contents are two green Gideon pocket Bibles, Mr. Farkas's business card, marking the spot in Colossians 3, and one pair of really big 1977 eyeglass frames!

God talks to you and me through words of confirmation. How? The written Word often coupled with unusual and very exciting circumstances and/or pastoral counsel, along with the impression of His passionate Holy Spirit, guide you purposefully in His will. As they converge together in one experience, you will sense their synergy in that moment, and later on, you will never forget their impact and importance in your life.

God talks with a variety of intimate and powerful expressions—including words of love, conviction, forgiveness, and confirmation. Please don't ignore, discount, or underestimate the frequency, familiarity, or passion with which God wants to talk to you!

CHAPTER 5

When God Talks to You

Since February 18, 1984, I've spent one hour a day with God, listening to Him and talking to Him in two-way, written conversations. I made this lifelong commitment, unsolicited, near the end of a youth worker's conference in the presence of just one person. For over twenty-five years, no matter where I am, I gather my Bible, a notebook, and a daily devotional, and get alone with God. Almost immediately, I hear Him talk to me in some familiar way.

The amount of time I spend with God—one hour—has never wavered, but the time of day is usually determined one day in advance, depending upon my travel schedule, the time zone, or my family life.

My rule of thumb is to spend the first uninterrupted hour of my day in an appointment with God—both talking and listening to Him. This supernatural yet discernible two-way conversation between God and man is often called prayer. By now you've probably noticed that I call these divinely human dialogues "God Talks."

This morning I awoke without an alarm at 5:30. Feeling as if I had been given a few extra hours in my day, I determined to get started on this chapter. I planned to write in the cozy warmth of the kitchen until my husband awoke and affectionately bugged me to join him for breakfast. After that break, I would help him get out the door, then get alone with God for an hour before getting back to my writing.

Apparently, this was not the right order for my day, because I repeatedly struggled to get my thoughts organized for this chapter. I knew what I wanted to say. I had gathered plenty of ideas and inspiring quotes to add sage advice, yet no matter how hard I tried, words just wouldn't flow.

Then, I asked, "Lord, what's wrong?" The thought followed, "You and I haven't had our alone time together yet today. You started your work on this chapter before WE even talked!"

This thought passed through my mind a few more times until I set aside all of my books and my computer and listened to God talk to me.

I began by opening up to today's reading in Oswald Chambers' daily devotional *My Utmost for His Highest*. I shouldn't have been surprised to read (though I did gasp): "If you cannot express yourself on any subject, struggle until you can. If you do not, someone will be all the poorer all the days of his life. Struggle to re-express some truth of God to yourself, and God will use that expression to someone else. . . . Try to state to yourself what you feel implicitly to be God's truth and give God a chance to pass it on to someone else through you."[1]

I share this with you as an example of how obvious God is when He talks to me. He is NOT elusive. He is SO present. He is ALWAYS ready to talk to me with words that encourage, press in, invite, and direct me.

In my rush to convince you that God talks, I neglected to address the all-too-common excuses that hinder us from hearing God talk.

When you are too busy, too tired, or too lazy to spend time alone with God, these excuses will become habits. They will inevitably and eventually steal your intimacy with God.

When you ignore and avoid God or keep Him waiting rather than making and keeping an appointment with Him, more often than not, you will:

> make impulsive decisions,
>> waste valuable time, and
>>> cause clarity to be elusive.

When you allow the tyranny of the urgent to steal away, interrupt, or sabotage your designated appointment with God (even when you're writing a book about hearing God talk), you will invariably spin around and around in circles.

My point? I should have known better.

Before you can address *when* God talks, you must consider the common hindrances that keep you from hearing God talk.

Common Hindrances to Hearing God Talk

It should be no surprise that the first hindrance to hearing God is doubt or unbelief. How can you hear God if you don't believe that He talks, that He exists, or that He loves you?

Doubt will deafen your ears and blind the eyes of your soul from hearing God talk. Unbelief will muffle and distort the sound of God's voice until you reject rather than experience His inner presence.

Dallas Willard, a modern-day philosopher, writes in *Hearing God:*

> We live in a culture that has, for centuries now, cultivated the idea that the *skeptical* person is always smarter than the one who believes. . . . Only a very hardy individualist or social rebel—or one desperate for another life—therefore stands any chance of discovering the substantiality of the spiritual life today.[2]

You must get over and get rid of any doubt or unbelief that keeps you from believing that God indeed speaks! The Bible is a book full of "God Talks." If you need convincing, open it anywhere and begin to read. In the psalms—which are the recorded two-way conversations between God and people—you see and hear the exchange between God and human beings. In each of the historical books of the Old Testament, and included in the letters of the prophets or disciples, are recorded the words that they heard God say to them.

From the beginning of time, men and women have heard God talk and recorded their conversations with Him.

So if you have never heard God talk, I encourage you to test God's willingness and ability to talk to you. I am confident He will prove to you that He desires to engage in a personal, conversational relationship with *you*. Or if you have heard God talk only occasionally and His voice remains elusive, don't despair! R. A. Torrey, author of numerous books, encourages you by saying, "Many of the most blessed seasons of prayer I have ever known have begun with the feeling of utter deadness and prayerlessness; but in my helplessness and coldness, I have cast myself upon God, and looked to Him to send His Holy Spirit to teach me to pray, and He has done it."[3]

The second and perhaps most common hindrance to hearing God talk is sin. Oswald Chambers, a devotional writer who doesn't mince words, wrote, "If a man cannot get through to God it is because there is a secret thing he does not intend to give up."[4]

Sin—an offense we commit against God and others—in most cases is obvious and very difficult to hide. (Of course, whether you admit or agree that you have committed an offense is another issue.) As in any relationship, selfish, impure motives or deceptive, hurtful actions will separate you from those you love. A consequence of sin is that it keeps you from hearing God's voice or receiving His insights and answers. Psalm 66:16–20 (emphasis added) puts it plainly:

> Come and listen, all you who fear God; let me tell you what he has done for me. I cried out to him with my mouth; his praise was on my tongue. *If I had cherished sin in my heart, the Lord would not have listened*; but God has surely listened and heard my voice in prayer. Praise be to God, who has not rejected my prayer or withheld his love from me!

A clean conscience and a pure heart will open the pathway for clear communication between two people who love each other.

A third hindrance to hearing God talk is poor time management. You will miss hearing God speak to you *if and when* you make everything or everyone else a greater priority in your life. You can call it busyness, or laziness, or sleepiness, but if you don't make time to be alone with God, your life will reflect His absence. (I'll discuss this more thoroughly in later chapters, but suffice it to say, hearing God talk requires time: planned, set aside, quiet time.)

Contemplative author and Catholic priest Henri Nouwen, in his classic book on solitude called *The Way of the Heart,* suggests that no person should be exempt from spending time alone with God. He writes, "The concrete shape of this discipline of solitude will be different for each person depending on individual character, ministerial task, and milieu. But a real discipline never remains vague or general. It is as concrete and specific as daily life itself."[5]

The fourth hindrance to hearing God talk is lack of interest in the secret life.

E. M. Bounds (1835–1913), a young lawyer turned pastor, wrote numerous books on "the business of praying," including *Purpose in Prayer.* Because he arose each morning at four to be alone with God, I find his words very credible. He writes, "Secret praying is the test, the gauge, the preserver of man's relation to

God. The prayer chamber, while it is the test of the sincerity of our devotion to God, becomes also the measure of the devotion. . . . The lingering to stay, the loathsomeness to leave, are values that we put on communion alone with God; they are the price we pay for the Spirit's hours of heavenly love."[6]

The secret life is not an invitation to dwell in numbness or emptiness.

But it does require silence.

Many, if not most of us, are just uncomfortable with silence. Some of us are even afraid of it. In *The Way of the Heart,* Nouwen reveals the unique perspective that the Desert Fathers held toward silence. These experts, who spent extended amounts of time alone with God, "did not think of solitude as being alone, but as being alone with God. They did not think of silence as not speaking, but as listening to God."[7]

I have found that when you quit negotiating your own way, incessantly talking, trying to manipulate any of your other options, or considering everyone else's suggestions, and finally turn your attention to God alone, you will hear Him talk.

When you have identified any hindrances that keep you from hearing God talk to you and resolve to remove them, you will be most prepared to hear God talk:

In the morning hour;
At any or every hour;
For one hour.

In the Morning Hour

King David wrote and recorded many of his intimate and personal conversations with God. In Psalm 5:3 he wrote, "In the morning, O Lord, you hear my voice; in the morning I lay my requests before you and wait in expectation."

Why the morning? Any businessperson, educator, corporate executive, or parent knows the secret of the morning—it remains the most uninterrupted time of your day. Others are sleeping. The technology hasn't begun transmitting. Nor have your companions, employees, or family members awakened to make specific requests for your time. It's quiet!

Andrew Murray, prolific writer on the secret to spending time alone with God, dedicated his book *The Inner Life* to the "morning watch." He wrote,

> Consider the morning watch now as the means to this great end: I want to secure absolutely the presence of Christ for the entire day, to do nothing that can interfere with it. I feel that my success for the day will depend upon the clearness and the strength of faith that seeks and finds and holds Him in the inner chamber. . . . Above everything else, it is this fixed determination to secure Christ's presence that will overcome the temptation to be unfaithful or superficial in the keeping of our pledge. It is this determination which will make the morning watch itself a mighty means of grace in strengthening character, and enabling us to say 'No' to every call for self-indulgence. . . . The Christian who makes personal devotion to Christ his watchword, will find in the morning hour that day by day insight into his holy calling is renewed.[8]

The "morning watch" was a significant habit for many of the greatest Christian men and women from every century.

One such historical figure was William Wilberforce (1759–1833), English philanthropist and abolitionist, who was devoted to long, quiet hours alone with God. E. M. Bounds shared a letter that Wilberforce wrote to his son:

> Let me implore you not to be seduced into neglecting, curtailing, or hurrying over your morning prayers. Of all things, guard against neglecting God in the prayer closet. There is nothing more fatal to the power of religion. More solitude and earlier

hours—prayer three times a day, at least. How much better might I serve if I cultivated a closer communion with God![9]

These words were written by a powerful political leader who was committed to God in all ways. As one whose days and nights were spent valiantly fighting to abolish slavery in England, Wilberforce's words reveal the source of his relentless ability to fight against evil in his culture: the morning hour.

I believe the morning hour alone with God is *still* the foundation of strength and power for any man or woman who is compelled to take up a just and noble cause.

God talks to you *at any time of any day*. But in the morning, as Isaiah the prophet discovered, "The Sovereign Lord has given me an instructed tongue, to know the word that sustains the weary. He wakens me morning by morning, wakens my ear to listen like one being taught" (50:4).

At Any and Every Hour

At the height of His exhausting itinerant ministry, Jesus made a habit of getting alone regularly to talk with God. Especially after long days of healing and preaching, as Luke 5:16 points out: "Jesus often withdrew to the wilderness for prayer" (NLT).

Resolved to receive God's counsel amidst the endless advice and suggestions of either His entourage or His enemies, very often, He would slip away into the night as is described in Luke 6:12: "One day soon afterward Jesus went up on a mountain to pray, and he prayed to God all night" (NLT).

Upon returning from this and other late-night or early-morning rendezvous with God, He would proceed to make prophetic statements, controversial decisions, or delegate unusual assignments to His disciples. After time alone with God, Jesus would unflinchingly share God's Word with others—no matter the consequences.

Late-night, all-night, or all-day prayer was not only a characteristic of Jesus' time with the Father. In the eighteenth century, the Moravian Church hosted a twenty-four-hours-a-day prayer movement that began in the small village of Herrnhut, Germany. Hours of unbroken prayer turned into days and were sustained for one hundred years (1727–1827) by a small community of three hundred men, women, and children. Imagine—24/7 prayer for one hundred years! Did spending unbroken time in conversation with God change them or the world? It probably changed both. History records that hundreds of missionaries were sent throughout the world during the first thirty years of their one hundred years of nonstop prayer.

The thought of setting aside one, two, three, or four hours alone with God seems unimaginable to many of us.

In a famous sermon, Charles Spurgeon, renowned pastor and founder of a pastor's college in England during the nineteenth century, challenged men and women to consider giving God just one night—*all night*—alone with God in prayer:

> What, have we no sacred ambition? Are we deaf to the yearnings of divine love? . . . Surely, brethren, if we have given whole days to folly, we can afford a space for heavenly wisdom. There was a time when we gave whole nights to . . . dancing and the world's revelry; we did not tire then. . . . Why do we grow weary when asked to watch with our Lord? Up, sluggish heart, Jesus calls you! Rise and go forth to meet the heavenly Friend in the place where He manifests Himself.[10]

Spurgeon's description of the gregarious, all-night partier could easily depict a twenty-first century man or woman. Most of us can't wait until Friday comes around each week. Many of us look forward to staying out late, dancing, playing sports, attending concerts, or just relaxing by hanging out with friends. We'll easily chat all night with our buddies in a coffee shop or on a road trip. And we love to cozy up on the couch with a rented movie into the wee hours of the morning, but we can hardly fathom giving God the same amount of time!

Why is it so difficult to be alone with God on a regular basis?

Why can't we spend *even one hour alone with God*?

For One Hour . . .

At least three different books that I am aware of capture the story of the *1947 Fellowship of the Burning Heart*. Each book tells the powerful story of four individuals who determined to spend no less than *one hour each day* alone with God as a lifetime commitment and how, over time, it impacted their lives and the lives of many others.

Bill Bright was one of those four. In the year 2000, I received a copy of his biography, *Amazing Faith,* from Vonette, his wife of more than fifty years. I was surprised to read of people and events I'd never heard of before. For example, Bright credits Henrietta Mears with greatly influencing his spiritual life. Researching Mears' intriguing life and her "big" personality consumed me over the next few weeks.

Henrietta was a preacher and teacher ahead of her time. She not only taught hundreds of collegians and young businesspersons at a large church in the Los Angeles area during the mid-1900s, but she also founded a Christian camp and publishing company that remain in operation today. But it was during the '40s and '50s that Mears profoundly impacted the lives of young Christian leaders of that era, such as Billy Graham, Louis Evans Jr., Richard Halverson, and Bill Bright, even sparking a national revival at American universities between 1947 and 1949.

Her biography, *Dream Big*, reveals a woman who possessed a deeply personal, boldly conversational relationship with God that was endearing to many and impressive to most.

Whether in small or large groups of men and women, Henrietta Mears would talk out loud to God, fearlessly yet casually. It was said, "She was never formal with God. She just spoke to Him as a person speaks to a friend, without worrying about grammar or niceties. The most prominent characteristic of her praying was her complete enthrallment with the person of Christ. She knew Him and He knew her; they were on speaking terms with each other and exercised this relationship freely."[11]

One night, after a particularly powerful camp meeting, Henrietta passionately called all in attendance to become wholly surrendered—sold out—to God. Her timely message captivated many who had grown disenchanted with the state of Christianity in America. Her words would not let them go. Unbeknownst to each other, a few of the men found their way to Henrietta's cabin later that night. In desperation, they spent all night talking to God. Three of the men who convened in her cabin were Bill Bright (at the time, a businessman); a youth pastor, Richard Halverson; and Louis Evans Jr., a pastor's son.

A chapter in *They Found the Secret,* dedicated to Richard Halverson's life, details in his own words the experience and impressions of that same memorable night:

> The way led past Miss Henrietta Mears's cabin; and here I was strangely constrained to enter and pray. . . . I began to pray, others followed, and God came down into that cabin. There was no unusual ecstatic or cataclysmic experience, but God visited us in a way none of us had known before. There was weeping and laughter, much talking and planning. What is most clear from that experience is the fact that upon the hearts of us who were in that prayer meeting was laid a burden for the world and a world-wide vision that persists to this day. . . . In the middle of the night I finally got to my cabin but could not sleep. Under real compulsion I spent time at the typewriter and wrote what later became known as the four commitments of *The Fellowship of the Burning Heart.*[12]

Bill Bright's account also gives the exact details of the four written commitments within their Burning Heart contract. Each resonated with me personally—purity, sobriety, and evangelism—but none as much as the first:

> I am committed to the principle that Christian discipleship is sustained solely by God alone through His Spirit; that the abiding life of John 15 is His way of sustaining me. *Therefore, I pledge myself to a disciplined devotional life in which I promise through prayer, Bible study, and devotional reading to give God not less than one continuous hour per day.*[13]

Amazing—how amazing!

Unaware of the *1947 Fellowship of the Burning Heart*, unsolicited, in 1984 I had made a similar commitment and have since used a similar pattern to spend not less than one hour a day alone with God.

Upon reading *Amazing Faith* in the summer of 2000, even though I had known the Brights for years, I was absolutely stunned to uncover their group's conviction to pray one hour a day. Why?

Since 1984, I've had quite a few people discourage me from spending one hour a day with God. Many have actually tried to dissuade me from talking about my commitment. I've even had spiritual leaders ask me *not* to challenge their group to spend one hour a day with God—stressing that I am only burdening them with a discipline that is nearly impossible to maintain. Others have suggested that I *forgo* asking people to designate a specific amount of time, or downplay the "two-way" conversation structure I use, or promote a more haphazard, spontaneous method of talking and listening to God (as if I didn't take into consideration the validity of spur-of-the-moment prayers).

And though I would agree that all of these ideas have some merit, when I read the story of the *1947 Fellowship of the Burning Heart*, I felt as if I had found my spiritual soul mates! I wondered if I had perhaps been born a few decades too late. I so deeply admired their devotional lives and how jealously they guarded them, yet I knew few contemporaries who embraced a similar conviction. After sixteen lonely years (at that time) of carrying a torch, I couldn't help but shout, "I'm 'in.' I've been 'in.' I'm staying 'in!' "

Granted, sixty minutes a day is *not* a lot of time. But when that—or any—specific amount of time is attached to God, it sounds impossibly long or much too demanding to request of the average person. Yet most of us spend at least one hour a day either watching television, working on the computer, or working out at the gym. Some of us spend even *more* than one hour a day in business or staff meetings.

If you're like me, God needs at least that much time to chisel, mold, purge, and prune you. If you're like me, one hour alone with God each day gives Him extended time to talk to you—to shape and reshape your life. In fact, one hour, on some days, may seem hardly enough time for Him to change your stubbornness, empower your weakness, heal your relationships, or even restore your soul.

One hour a day with God, as the *1947 Fellowship of the Burning Heart* discovered, is where the seed of an idea turns into an organization and millions are changed for eternity (such as Bill Bright's Campus Crusade for Christ International); where an amazing prayer is uttered from a mountaintop, resulting in unaffordable property being purchased at a rock-bottom price (such as Henrietta Mears's founding of Forest Home Campground); and where a young California pastor eventually finds the confidence to become the chaplain to the U.S. Senate for fourteen years (such as Richard Halverson, Chaplain of the Senate from 1981–1995).

During the 2008 Olympic coverage, sportscaster Jimmy Roberts—speaking of Michael Phelps, the Olympic athlete who had just won the most gold medals in the history of the modern

Olympics—said, "The stakes and standards for the truly great are different."

I consider the standard—to spend *not less than one hour a day* talking to and listening to God—set by the *1947 Fellowship of the Burning Heart* not a burden, but a path to follow, which has been traveled by some of history's greatest men and women.

I'm living proof that spending one hour a day with God certainly won't hurt you! In fact, I have found that each hour spent alone with God—talking and listening—becomes an immovable building block in a solid foundation in your personal and conversational relationship with Him.

When God Talks, Will You Be Listening?

God talks *to you* always. He is unchanging, unrelenting, and indomitable in His desire to communicate with you. He is everpresent. God talks to you . . .

> in the morning, noon, and night
> from the day you were born until the day you die
> in the good times and in the bad times
> whether you are listening or not.

God reaches out to talk to you through every natural and supernatural means available. And He waits for you to respond.

Oswald Chambers makes the case, "Not often, but every once in a while, God brings us to a major turning point—a great crossroads in our life. From that point we either go toward a more and more slow, lazy, and useless Christian life, or we become more and more on fire."[14]

Perhaps God is talking to you right now.

CHAPTER 6

Increase Your Desire for Hearing God Talk

It happens if you let it. Love fades.

In 1976, at twenty-one years old, I was incredibly passionate about God. I was uncontrollably bubbly and outspoken about my relationship with Him as a forgiving Father, a sacrificial Savior, and a dynamic spiritual force coming into my heart and turning *all of me* toward *all of Him*. I think my enthusiasm for God was even irritating to some people. But sadly, by the time I was only twenty-nine years old, I was simply going through the motions of talking all *about* God, but not talking *with* Him. My relationship with God had grown passionless and stagnant.

I didn't actually know what was missing in my life until I attended a conference where godly men and women shared their very personal and exciting stories of what happened when they spent time alone with God. Though they had known Him for decades, they still expressed a deep and passionate love relationship with God.

At first I was jealous. (I know . . . that's not a good sign.) But my jealousy quickly turned away from wanting what they had into more of a longing for my own passion toward God to be revived. I reminisced about my wildly exciting early years of knowing God, when I trusted Him completely, expected Him to do the impossible, and talked with Him about every little thing!

Each consecutive presentation at the conference built on the next until I could hear the message loud and clear: Prayerlessness was the cause of my apathy and complacency toward God.

Not only was my relationship with God suffering because of it, but every area of my life was being negatively impacted. (I was overweight, habitually tardy for meetings, a procrastinator, jealous of others who were skinnier and richer than me—which included most people—and I was easily angered, especially toward my toddler.)

By exposing three lies I had believed, these leaders dramatically changed the way I *felt* about spending time alone with God.

Lies Exposed

Initially, they dispelled the notion that God *needed me* to work for Him. They taught—and I believed them—that God wanted me, first and foremost, to talk and listen to Him every day. They spoke of how much God loved them, how often He talked to them—giving them affirmation, ideas, and important messages for themselves and others. Not one of them spoke about their successful ministries without attaching their stories to hours or even months of personal and/or corporate prayer. Without trying to impress us, or even caring about what we—the younger generation—thought, they said, "You'll never be greater than your prayer life." This convicted me. (If someone asked me to respond, I would have answered, "What prayer life?")

Second, these men and women were thirty and forty years older than me. At the time, my peers and I rarely read books by dead people. We were most often attracted to the newest and most innovative ideas, authors, or speakers. And I, in particular, felt that those who were older (or dead) were outdated and irrelevant. But the maturity of the conference speakers, all seasoned leaders, proved that experience was an advantage—they had proven track records! The depth and wealth of their knowledge about the "inner life" was refreshing and appealing and humbling. Even more inspiring were their amazing stories of answers to prayer, moving me from stagnation to motivation. I realized that both excitement and adventure had been missing in my relationship with God for too many years. I connected the dots—too little time alone with God equaled too little passion for God.

Third, they pointed out and blew away all of my misconceptions about prayer (such as: Prayer is what you do when you're too old to work; prayer meetings are for those with the "gift" of prayer; or "one" prayer isn't enough to change something). They tore them apart. None were left. I had no recourse. They made me hungry for God. They showed the way *to* Him was to be *with* Him. I could no longer make excuses for my laziness. I determined to do whatever it took to get alone with God daily. I wanted more and more and more of God in my life.

They reminded me—and I've never forgotten—that when you love someone, you are no longer content just knowing them, *you want to be with them.*

In each of the previous chapters, we've answered important questions such as:

> to whom God talks,
> why God talks,
> how God talks,
> what God says, and
> when God talks.

Though intellectual understanding will certainly expand your knowledge of God, a personal and conversational relationship with God will consistently fan the flame of your *desire* and *passion* to know Him more intimately.

A Template for Increasing Your Desire for God

David's devotion to and intimacy with God as expressed in Psalm 139 has been a template for thousands of years, showing us *how* to wholeheartedly love God by passionately and humbly communicating with Him. It includes an assortment of conversational styles, including confession, profession of faith, pleas for help, and praises to the Lord. King David's wide variety of expressions transport you immediately into the depths of his most personal and intimate relationship with God.

As you read each portion of this psalm, paraphrase or personalize any words from each sentence or stanza that have a similar or special meaning to you by exchanging David's words with your own.

> O Lord, you have examined my heart
>   and know everything about me.
>   You know when I sit down or stand up.
>   You know my thoughts even when I'm far away.
>   You see me when I travel
>   and when I rest at home.
>   You know everything I do.
>   You know what I am going to say
>   even before I say it, Lord.
>   You go before me and follow me.
>   You place your hand of blessing on my head.
>   Such knowledge is too wonderful for me,
>   too great for me to understand!

I can never escape from your Spirit!
    I can never get away from your presence!
If I go up to heaven, you are there;
    if I go down to the grave, you are there.
If I ride the wings of the morning,
    if I dwell by the farthest oceans,
even there your hand will guide me,
    and your strength will support me.
I could ask the darkness to hide me
    and the light around me to become night—
but even in darkness I cannot hide from you.
    To you the night shines as bright as day.
    Darkness and light are the same to you.

You made all the delicate, inner parts of my body
    and knit me together in my mother's womb.
Thank you for making me so wonderfully complex!
    Your workmanship is marvelous—how well I
    know it.
You watched me as I was being formed
    in utter seclusion,
    as I was woven together in the dark of the
    womb.
You saw me before I was born.
    Every day of my life was recorded in your book.
Every moment was laid out
    before a single day had passed.

How precious are your thoughts about me, O God.
    They cannot be numbered!
I can't even count them;
    they outnumber the grains of sand!
And when I wake up,
    you are still with me! . . .

Search me, O God, and know my heart;
    test me and know my anxious thoughts.

> Point out anything in me that offends you,
> > and lead me along the path of everlasting life. (vv.
> 1–18, 23–24 NLT)

If you want to grow in intimacy toward God, to increase your desire for Him, follow David's example by:

- Inviting Him regularly to speak into your heart
- Being always aware of His presence
- Getting "in tune" with Him
- Committing to His Sovereignty
- Understanding that you are special to Him
- Listening to everything He has to say
- Letting Him restore your soul

Invite God to Come Into Your Heart

David is vulnerable with God. He lets Him in. As if opening his palms to the sky, he welcomes God into the secret places of his heart with a verbal invitation.

> O Lord, you have examined my heart
> > and know everything about me.
>
> > > PSALM 139:1 NLT

I doubt if you could name more than a handful of persons—if any—with whom you regularly share your innermost joys and fears, failings and successes, or tell your every secret thought. It's just too risky to be that transparent with someone *unless* you know them very well, trust them very much, or have loved them for a very long time. You just don't let people "in" if you think they are going to shame you or abandon you.

It's impressive how David initiates intimacy with God by immediately asking Him to examine his innermost thoughts. He lets God enter into the place where few of us are willing to invite people to come in. David's intimate invitation speaks volumes of his personal relationship with God and begs the question "How comfortable are you in your conversational relationship with God?"

Rosalind Rinker (1906–2002), Asbury graduate, Inter-Varsity staff member, and author of *Prayer: Conversing With God*, believed that the more conversational your relationship with God, the more "real" God would become to you. She described her conversations with God as "a dialogue between two persons who love each other."[1]

Those who exchange their innermost thoughts with each other obviously know each other better than those who speak less often, only occasionally, or intermittently. Thus friendly, warm, and deep conversations provide "real" opportunities to build intimacy.

For every page written, every book authored, and every sermon preached by Oswald Chambers, his simplest description of his relationship with God is revealed in this quote: "Get into the habit of saying, 'Speak, Lord,' and life will become a romance."[2]

King David, Rosalind Rinker, and Oswald Chambers presented their intense love for God not as unattainable or unapproachable but as available to anyone willing to invite Him into their hearts. Not wanting to grow stagnant, they increased their love for God by engaging in intimate, two-way conversations with Him. This built their trust in God, enough to enthusiastically and often invite Him to come into the known place where all love is tested—the heart.

For many of you, your first "real" conversation with God started with the words "Come into my heart." And if you are like me, it was an invitation that changed everything about you for the better!

If you want to continually increase in intimacy—familiarity, closeness, and affection—toward God, make it a daily habit to say the words "Come into my heart, Father. Come into my heart, Lord Jesus. Come into my heart, Holy Spirit." Open your palms and lift your eyes to the sky and say, "Keep coming. . . ." Be vulnerable.

Acknowledge God's Ever-Presence

David never lost sight of God.

David's written conversations with God kept them in each other's presence. He said (and I paraphrase), "You know all about

Let God Talk to You

Prepare Your Heart for "God Talks"

Up until this chapter, I've been telling you all about how God talks to me. Now it's your turn. Hearing God talk takes time and practice. Throughout the rest of the book you'll find sections labeled **Let God Talk to You**. They will give you ideas to jump-start your conversation with God. Some ideas may work well for you, and others may not. I've purposely designed these experiences to be experimental so that you might find a lifelong pattern for your own "God Talks."

In this chapter, there is an experience for each portion of Psalm 139. Take each component and either answer the questions or write a response that includes poetry, a favorite chorus or song, a specific Bible verse, or a personal prayer.

Invite God Into Your Heart

In your own words, invite God to come into your heart. You're most likely at home, so be as comfortable and current with God as possible—not thinking about the past or the future—just be in the moment.

Topics to help you get started include: If you have been distant from God, tell Him why. If you miss God and want to renew your friendship, tell Him so. If you have doubts about Him, express them.

Phrases to help you get started include: "Come in, dear Jesus. . . . Father, I need you. . . . I want to know you better, Holy Spirit. . . ."

me! You know when I sit and stand and speak. You know when I travel or rest. You go before and behind me."

By acknowledging God's presence at all times and in all places, David was safe. He knew there was nowhere he could go without God's knowledge of his whereabouts.

Little churchgoing children learn numerous stanzas to the song "Oh, Be Careful Little Eyes" in order to teach them about the invisible God, helping them to conceptualize that He sees, knows, and hears them, even though they can't see Him:

> Oh, be careful little eyes, what you see
>> Oh, be careful little eyes, what you see
>
> *For the Father up above,*
>> *Is looking down in love,*
>> So be careful little eyes,
>> what you see.
>
> Oh, be careful little ears, what you hear, (repeat)
>> Oh, be careful little mouth, what you say, (repeat),
>> Oh, be careful little hands, what you do (repeat),
>> Oh, be careful little feet, where you go (repeat),
>> Oh, be careful little mind, what you think (repeat),
>
> Oh, be careful little heart, what you love
>> Oh, be careful little heart, what you love
>
> *For the Father up above,*
>> *Is looking down in love,*
>> So be careful little heart,
>> what you love.[3]

As one who is married, I completely understand how to acknowledge my husband's existence even when he is not physically with me. It's very practical: I am faithful to my spouse when we are not together. I *act* as if I'm married even when we're apart. I wear a ring that reminds me and shows others that I am "taken." And because

I know my husband loves me, is counting on or rooting for me even when we're not together, I proceed accordingly. I have a conscious understanding that he owns my heart. He is always present with me, though not visible to others—whether I'm on an airplane, at a hotel, working at the office, or shopping at the mall.

It is similar with God. He is always with us, but because we can't see Him, it's easy to forget He's there. Being with God can be very practical. Here are just a few ideas:

> Speak to Him as you leave your house each day. Say, "I know you go before and behind me, Lord. Thank you for your protection."

> Picture Him in line with you at the post office, or seated next to you in the car during a traffic jam, or looking over your shoulder while writing an email to anyone!

Acknowledging God's presence *in any given moment* will heighten your attention both to His presence and any inappropriate words, emotions, or actions. Instantly, you'll be inspired to reach for higher standards; you'll want to make Him proud of you.

Let God Talk to You

Acknowledge God's Presence

God wants to be with you. Describe the last time you felt God's presence. Were you inside a building or outside enjoying nature? Was someone talking to you when a thought popped into your head or were you alone? Share the experience as if you were writing to a dear, but long-distance friend. Tell your friend what it felt like to be with God. Or draw a picture or create a painting that shows what this experience would be like. (If you've never felt God's presence, express how you would feel right now if God walked into the room. What would you say and/or do?)

Dallas Willard, in *Hearing God,* writes, "God wants to be wanted, to be wanted enough that we are *ready,* predisposed to find him present with us."[4]

When you acknowledge His constant companionship, loneliness cannot consume you, fear cannot overtake you, and worry cannot overwhelm you.

Get "In Tune" With God

For a variety of reasons, Rosalind Rinker is one of my spiritual mentors. Decades apart, she and I have written books on a similar subject: prayer. Because we shared a similar, simple method for making a difficult spiritual discipline so tangible, it made me both her fan and student! She taught others to converse out loud with God; I take a different approach and teach people to record their two-way conversations with God in writing.

We both agree—prayer is not simply talking to God, nor is it only listening to God. It is a divinely human conversation that connects us emotionally, spiritually, and physically with the invisible God.

Rinker's following timeless teaching helps you get "in tune" with God.

Begin by becoming aware of Him right where you are.

Then take turns talking with Him about *one subject at a time.* Focus on a specific issue or concern and talk with God about it *until you feel the discussion comes to a conclusion.*

Don't interrupt. Let God talk first while you listen.

Then talk to Him, sharing your thoughts and feelings; picture Him listening to you.[5]

"God Talks" are not monologues but dialogues.

You can quickly get "in tune" with God by engaging in a conversational pattern with Him—both talking and listening. To know Him better, to grow in intimacy with God, it is essential to exchange ideas, share aspirations, and discuss important decisions, just as you would converse with anyone.

King David learned, just as you and I can, that he didn't even need to speak a word and God already knew what he was going to say. They were deeply "in tune" with each other.

As often as possible, make David's words your own:

> You know what I am going to say
> even before I say it, Lord.
> You go before me and follow me.
> You place your hand of blessing on my head.
> Such knowledge is too wonderful for me,
> too great for me to understand!
>
> PSALM 139:4–6 NLT

Commit to God's Sovereignty

David was convinced that no amount of darkness or trouble could keep him from hearing God's voice. Over and over, this provided comfort to David, increasing His trust in God. He wrote,

Let God Talk to You

Stay "In Tune" With Each Other

As suggested by Rosalind Rinker, choose one specific concern or issue and discuss your thoughts about it with God—what is not working, what you ultimately hope to accomplish, why you feel that you are stuck—then listen for God's response. Write down the complete back-and-forth conversation. Example: He said, I said. Share the result of this exercise with a spiritual mentor and ask for her input.

I can never escape from your Spirit!
    I can never get away from your presence!
If I go up to heaven, you are there;
    if I go down to the grave, you are there.
If I ride the wings of the morning,
    if I dwell by the farthest oceans,
even there your hand will guide me,
    and your strength will support me.
I could ask the darkness to hide me
    and the light around me to become night—
but even in darkness I cannot hide from you.
    To you the night shines as bright as day.
Darkness and light are the same to you.

PSALM 139:7–12 NLT

I doubt anyone will be able to convince you of God's sovereignty—that He is who He says He is. You will have to test it and try it until you believe it for yourself.

There are a variety of ways to do this.

First, you gain confidence in God's sovereignty through your own experiences with Him. They are indisputable proof to you, as they are to me, that God is able to save, that He is trustworthy, all-powerful, all-knowing, and all-wise.

A second way to bolster your belief in God's sovereignty is to study, review, and research the Bible for yourself. For example, if you yearly read the Bible from cover to cover, your knowledge of God will become your own, not based on what others have told you the Bible says. The more you study God's Word, the more clearly you will recognize His voice, and the more prone you will be to believe in God's sovereignty rather than chance or luck.

Another method I've used to increase my understanding of God is to both memorize and meditate on individual verses in the Bible, such as this passage in Zephaniah 3:17:

For the Lord your God is living among you.
    He is a mighty savior.

He will take delight in you with gladness.
With his love, he will calm all your fears.
He will rejoice over you with joyful songs. (NLT)

I encourage you to hold on to, and even post in plain view, any verses that encourage your faith, deepen your love, or bolster your confidence in the God who loves you.

Throughout the Bible, hundreds of written conversations between God and His followers are recorded, and the outcomes of their lives are on display. The two-way conversations between God and Daniel, David, Jesus, and Mary are compelling examples of how to cling to God, especially when you cannot see Him or in the face of crushing disappointment.

Innumerable historical accounts are recorded of those who knew God and loved Him over the centuries—like Hudson Taylor or George Müller—whose faith overcame impossible odds to achieve unbelievable feats upon hearing God talk to them. Each person, each story, each account can bolster your faith that God is who He says He *is*.

My conviction, like David's, allows me to trust God's ability to save or rescue me, and allows me to hear Him talk to me, *especially* when I'm afraid. (And believe me, I'm afraid more than I care to admit!) In those dark moments and even in dark seasons, I have never, ever doubted that God is able to rescue me by *somehow* lifting me out of the darkness that is attempting to swallow me up.

One such time was when my husband was diagnosed with prostate cancer. Daily, it would have been easy to succumb to the negative thoughts and dwell on the possible devastating outcomes of this disease. Yet by beginning each morning in an appointment with God, purposely acknowledging His sovereignty—that He sees and knows everything about us, and that He guides us—my husband and I were daily carried through three long years of living with cancer.

My strong commitment to the belief that God is sovereign has not only bolstered *my* faith, but I know it has given others strength as well. I receive emails and letters regularly from strangers who have been encouraged by the way I have prayed for them weeks, months, or years before God answered my prayers. Others call or write my office to share how my "answers to prayer" encouraged them to persevere when they were temporarily weak in faith, or how my stories gave them courage to call on God to answer their requests.

We're not "more spiritual" than others when God answers our specific requests or meets our deepest needs. We do, though, become powerful witnesses to others of God's sovereignty and that He is who He says He is.

Let God Talk to You

Commit Yourself to His Sovereignty

Develop an ongoing list of your most favorite and/or meaningful Bible verses and give one reason/sentence why you chose each verse. In addition, comment on how God used each verse or passage to change your course of direction or encourage you if/when you were weary, or why you think He wanted you to hold on and/or put your hope in this verse.

Understand That You Are Special to God

David acknowledged that God knew Him before his life began. He acknowledged that he was special to God:

> You made all the delicate, inner parts of my body
> and knit me together in my mother's womb.
> Thank you for making me so wonderfully complex!
> Your workmanship is marvelous—how well I
> know it.
> You watched me as I was being formed
> in utter seclusion,

as I was woven together in the dark of the womb.
You saw me before I was born.
Every day of my life was recorded in your book.
Every moment was laid out
before a single day had passed.

PSALM 139:13–16 NLT

Thousands of years later, Rick Warren, pastor of Saddleback Church, essentially said the same thing in his forty-day adventure, *The Purpose-Driven Life.*

Day Two (the second chapter) of his forty-day adventure is titled, "You Are Not an Accident." It opens with the words of God: "I am your Creator. You were in my care even before you were born" (Isaiah 44:2a CEV).

Warren then begins this chapter in his own approachable words, saying:

> You are not an accident. Your birth was no mistake or mishap, and your life is no fluke of nature. Your parents may not have planned you, but God did. He was not at all surprised by your birth. In fact, he expected it. Long before you were conceived by your parents, you were conceived in the mind of God. He thought of you first. It is not fate, nor chance, nor luck, nor coincidence that you are breathing at this very moment. . . . God prescribed every single detail of your body. He deliberately chose your race, the color of your skin, your hair, and every other feature.[6]

Rick Warren really nailed it, didn't he? *The Purpose-Driven Life* has sold over twenty-five million copies not because of a fluke or a fad but because it answers the questions *everyone* asks: "Who am I? Why am I here?"

Why have millions read *The Purpose-Driven Life*, studied it in small groups, and shared it with others? Everyone wants to be loved. Everyone wants to know they are special. Everyone wants to believe they were created for a purpose and that their life has meaning. (If you haven't read it, you should. At its conclusion, you'll be hard-pressed to ever again believe that you are not special to God!)

I am especially encouraged with the unique style that Rick Warren uses throughout *The Purpose-Driven Life* when he quotes God's recorded words from the Bible. He doesn't make reference to a Scripture verse; instead he offers God's conversational words to the reader, saying:

> God says, "I have carried you since you were born; I have taken care of you from your birth. Even when you are old, I will be the same. Even when your hair has turned gray, I will take care of you. I made you and will take care of you."[7]

From before your birth until after you die, God talks to you, telling you He loves you and wants to be with you. Once you believe how special you are to God, I am confident you'll anticipate talking to God, and even make time every day to let God talk to you.

Listen to Every Little Thing God Has to Say to You

David considered *everything* that God said to him—all of His thoughts toward him—to be precious and significant. Grasping

Let God Talk to You

Understand How Special You Are to God

Reread Rick Warren's "You Are Not an Accident" entry. Write down how it made you feel when you read the paragraph about God's special love toward you. Next, develop a timeline of your life from birth to present. Make a note of the significant times—few or many—that God made himself known to you, used you to help another person, gave you a special gift, answered a specific prayer, or opened a door for you to enter. Share this timeline with someone else.

this very simple concept will go a long way in increasing your affection toward God.

David marveled at how often, how much, and how many times God spoke to him during the day. In fact, he awoke expecting God's voice, welcoming him into another day.

> How precious are your thoughts about me, O God.
> > They cannot be numbered!
> I can't even count them;
> > they outnumber the grains of sand!
> And when I wake up,
> > you are still with me!

> PSALM 139:17–18 NLT

Is that how you feel? Do you hear God's thoughts running through your mind from the moment you wake up until you hit the pillow each night?

Perhaps you have entertained the thought that God only speaks to people who have important positions. Or that He doesn't waste time speaking to average people about everyday, non-life-threatening matters. Perhaps you have brushed off an affirming thought that is full of loving parental pride, simply because it wasn't spoken by a human being. Or maybe you're avoiding God, expecting Him to scold you when you finally do get alone with Him.

God wants you to know what He's thinking! Psalm 25:14 says, "The Lord confides in those who fear him; he makes his covenant known to them."

Here are a few simple suggestions for increasing the frequency of your communication with Him:

When you hear God affirm you, say, "Thank you, Lord!"

When you hear God correct you, say, "I'm sorry, Lord!"

When you hear God direct you, say, "I'm going right now, Lord!"

Let God Talk to You

Listen to *Every Little Thing* He Has to Say

Today, try kneeling prayer. Before getting into bed, get on your knees and ask God to talk to you. On a notepad by your bed record the last words you hear God say before you doze off and the first words He says to you when you awake in the morning. If you initially don't hear God talk to you, try this experiment for a few days in a row or until you hear His voice.

When you hear God ask you to lift your chin to the sky, say, "I'm looking up, Lord!"

When you hear God whisper, "Cut it out," say, "I quit, Lord!"

When you finally understand that God expresses His endlessly deep thoughts and passionate feelings of love toward you *all throughout each day*, you'll become quite expectant . . . and perhaps even quite chatty!

Let God Restore and Renew Your Soul

David so deeply trusted God that he gave Him permission to examine his anxious thoughts, expose any impure motives, and not only change but remove any offensive ways from him.

I know this procedure well. For over twenty-five years, I've daily chosen to write these very words in my journal and wait for God to speak to me:

> Search me, O God, and know my heart;
>   test me and know my anxious thoughts.

Point out anything in me that offends you,
and lead me along the path of everlasting life.

PSALM 139:23–24 NLT

Not a single day has gone by when God hasn't gently pointed out or blatantly exposed one or more of my anxious thoughts, impure motives, or offensive actions that needed to come under His power. Not one day.

Frankly, no one can cut to the chase like God. No one can lay it out exactly as it is and still somehow convince you that whatever it is that you've done wrong, it simply isn't enough to make Him stop loving you. And no matter what inappropriate thing you've done or said, He is quick to give you innovative (though often humbling) ideas on how to restore or resolve the situation. No one but God can show you your "stuff" and make it look so ugly and yet so conquerable all at the same time. (In fact, just imagine how much money you'd save in counseling fees if you took your "God Talks" more seriously!)

I am convinced that it will be during your most honest conversations with God—those moments in which you let your guard down completely and humble yourself—that you will receive both the courage and power necessary to make seemingly impossible changes.

Surrender of self is the gateway to intimacy with God. Oswald Chambers, in describing the most God-changing moments in his life, said, "The Spirit of God seizes me and I am compelled to get alone with God and fight the battle before Him. Until I do this, I will lose every time."[8]

After All This Time . . .

It's been over twenty-five years since older, godly men and women convinced me that the Christian life is not meant to be lived without prayer—just as life itself is not meant to be lived without

Let God Talk to You

Let Him Wash Over You With His Love to Restore Your Soul

Set aside thirty minutes sometime during the coming week when you will have significant privacy and the assurance that you won't be interrupted. In advance of that scheduled appointment, locate five or more of your favorite worship CDs and make a note of the particular songs you like most on each CD and/or make a playlist of them on your iPod. Then, during your designated thirty minutes, play those tunes as loud as is appropriate—dance and laugh and sway and sing at the top of your lungs, praising God. Let God's love and words wash over you!

God. I have to admit, when I first heard these seasoned leaders speak, I was in my twenties. Prior to that conference, I had been either too lazy or too busy to make daily time with God a priority. But because their passion for God had not faded after decades of knowing and serving Him, I was drawn to their undeniable courage and strong faith. Their conversational relationships with God compelled me to want what they had. It was so appealing that my attitude instantly changed, and I still remain greatly influenced by them today.

Perhaps you are younger, and my call to "let God talk to you" is having the same impact on you. Or perhaps you've been a Christian for a while and you can almost hear God asking, even pleading with you to give Him more of yourself, more of your time. If so, I beg you to surrender yourself so that . . .

> One day you, too, will be the older one. Recording your two-way conversations with God provides you with an endless stack of stories and amazing answers to prayer that can't help but motivate others to pray.

> One day you will be the one teaching others the consequences of prayerlessness by sharing your failures or missteps.

One day you can prove that being chiseled and molded and changed by God's sculpting hands during hours alone with Him won't crush you, it'll just make you better . . . looking (kidding).

One day you will be the one who determinedly promotes the benefits of balancing discipline with devotion to God, because you know that *love fades if you let it.*

Don't let your love for God fade.
Daily . . .

- Invite Him into your heart.
- Acknowledge His presence.
- Stay "in tune" with Him.
- Commit yourself to His sovereignty.
- Understand how special you are to Him.
- Listen to *every little thing* He has to say.
- Let His love wash over you and restore your soul.

CHAPTER 7

Develop the Discipline of Hearing God Talk

> Our compulsive, wordy, and mind-oriented world has a firm grip on us, and we need a very strong and persistent discipline not to be squeezed to death by it.
>
> Henri Nouwen[1]

Discipline is not a very hip icon of the twenty-first century. In fact, for decades our culture has been characterized by time-saving, calorie-reducing, age-defying, money-growing shortcuts designed to replace hard work or decrease the need for self-control. We don't chase after a more disciplined life; we chase after anything that offers us more freedom!

So even though I know the backlash and arguments attached to a word that inherently promises sacrifice and surrender, I am still compelled to ask you to consider developing the discipline of hearing God talk.

Why am I so adamant?

First, I'm most concerned that if you hang on to mis-conceptions or excuses (such as, "God wouldn't want me to pray if I don't feel like it" or "Prayer is for the elderly") or ignore the consequences resulting from lack of prayer and discount its benefits, *you'll fail to hear God talk to you at a critical turning point in your life.*

Second, I fear that if you skip this chapter, gloss over it, or consciously refuse to develop the necessary disciplines to hear God talk, you'll actually be choosing the opposite: laziness, power-lessness, self-centeredness, and chaos.

Third, because I have found the combination of discipline *and* devotion to be equal companions in my most intimate relation-ships, I believe I am giving you good advice.

Finally, if you develop the discipline of hearing God talk to you, over time, I am confident you *will* experience the freedom that comes from possessing a safe and intimate conversational relationship with Him.

Hearing God talk is . . .

> a skill,
>> an art,
>>> a virtue,
>>>> an appointment,
>>>>> a practice, and
>>>>>> a commitment.

Hearing God Talk Is a Skill

There are at least three levels of listening.

The first level of listening is *spontaneous*. It doesn't require much effort. For example, when you hear shouts or sounds of warning you're startled. Most everyone pays attention to a blar-ing horn or a siren.

The second level of listening is *selective.* The television or radio can be turned on, transmitting conversations, interviews, or news, but unless you choose to listen, you won't hear anything.

The third level of listening is *intentional.* Those involved in personal or intimate relationships—parents, spouses, co-workers, siblings, or friends—will sooner or later have to engage in intentional listening.

As a pastor and a licensed counselor, my husband, Roger, primarily helps people become better communicators so they will experience more fulfilling, productive, and meaningful relationships! He loves the unlovely, is patient with those who make really stupid mistakes—including me—and is a mentor to hundreds of couples who are either engaged or married. He regularly teaches the benefits of developing a disciplined, respectful approach to listening to each other. He calls it *intentional listening.*

He teaches couples who are dating, engaged, or married how to intentionally listen to each other by:

- taking turns talking and listening;
- not interrupting while the other is talking;
- identifying the other person's thoughts and feelings;
- clarifying what they heard by repeating what they heard;
- asking the other person if they "got it right."

Intentional listening sounds like a lot of exhausting, clarifying, repetitive work, doesn't it? But this disciplined style of listening cultivates deeper, more fulfilling relationships.

My husband also teaches a conflict-resolution system to pre-married couples, reminding them that intentional listening skills not only are useful in sharing our deepest feelings but also serve as protection. Effective communication provides safe methods for not hurting each other with impulsive accusations, withdrawal, or isolation. Roger firmly advocates that young couples make every effort to allow discipline to fan the flame of desire, devotion, and passion in their lives.

Intimacy in any personal relationship, *including your relationship with God*, requires that you develop the difficult skill—sometimes tedious, sometimes frustrating, sometimes humiliating—of intentional listening. This type of listening is not a recreational exercise full of laughter and anecdotes. Most often, intentional listening is used to resolve a conflict or address another's hurt or concern. Perhaps that is why many of us steer away from more serious, transparent conversations with others.

During an evening church service, one of my pastors shared a very candid conversation he recently had with God. He told how it developed during two encounters. In the first conversation, he heard God say, "You're a liar and a manipulator." It was initially humorous, in a self-deprecating way. Then he told us, "I told God, 'No, I'm not *really* a liar. I just didn't want to hurt the person. I just changed a few details; it was a little thing.' " We all kind of chuckled. He continued his story, mentioning that a few weeks later, while alone with God, he heard the same words: "You're a liar and a manipulator." (Even writing this story, it sounds so harsh, yet this is honestly how he told it to us.) During this second conversation, after hearing God repeat the same comment, my pastor humbly answered Him, saying, "You're right. I am. It was wrong of me. Oh, forgive me." My pastor told us that after the initial shock of shame came over him, it was followed by an immediate sense of healing and forgiveness. His communication with God had been intimate, real, direct, and yet it didn't condemn him. It moved him toward God and gave him every positive reason to change his behavior.

Maybe that's why intentional listening is such a hard skill to acquire. The very exercise that promises intimacy, freedom, and victory—requires surrender.

In order to become an intentional listener with the invisible God—to listen and *not* talk while He is talking to me or to willingly set aside time to address a conflict or concern (rather than ignore it or Him)—I've kept a daily, written record of our two-way conversations, which I call my "God Talks." This simple habit has helped me overcome significant obstacles, including my resistance to silence, the powerful lure of entertainment, and my love of sleep. (I don't even attempt to listen to God with my eyes closed—I'm sure I'll fall asleep!)

Of course, writing out the words you hear God say (or that you say to Him) is certainly not a new idea. The Bible is full of "God Talks." The psalms especially—all 150 of them—are the written records of personal conversations human beings had with God.

If you have never heard God talk personally, honestly, and transparently to you, begin by acquiring the skill of intentional listening. Just as in my husband's premarital classes, intentional listening is a skill that must be learned, and takes practice. And because it doesn't come easy or feel natural to anyone to submit one's soul to a searchlight, it requires that you make an appointment—with a counselor, spiritual director, your spouse, or God—for certain conversations that might be uncomfortable. Ultimately, intentional listening is designed to increase your intimacy with someone you love or want to know better.

If you long for this kind of back-and-forth conversation with God, keep reading!

Hearing God Talk Is an Art

Art, in any form—music, sculpture, painting, or pencil drawing—creates an expression of what its creator sees, thinks, and feels.

God himself is an artist—every mountain, cloud, star, sunset, or ocean wave is designed to take your breath away. John Stott, author and theologian, sent a Christmas greeting to a friend that said, "The Bible is the Father's portrait of the Son, painted by the Holy Spirit."

I'd like to propose an alternative method for developing the discipline of hearing God talk to you: Turn your "God Talks" into works of art.

Use every manner of communication available to you—poetry, songs, journal writing, letter writing, drawing or photography, finding illustrations or metaphors—to record your two-way conversations with God.

First, choose your artistic elements:

> an easy-flowing pen or an especially thin-leaded pencil
> a journal with blank, graph, or lined pages
> a paper tablet
> a ringed loose-leaf refillable leather binder
> a canvas on an easel
> watercolors
> colored pens and pencils
> (always have extra supplies on hand)

If it takes a while for you to find a creative element or comfortable pattern through which you can regularly engage in two-way conversations with God, keep experimenting. If you get bored easily, change it up with variety!

For me, having a great roller-ball pen, a refillable journal, and a reliable system for talking and listening to God has kept me in the daily rhythm of conversing with God. I no longer spend valuable time looking for the next best idea on how to connect with Him.

Once you find the elements that work best for engaging your unique personality in "God Talks," I encourage you to stick with them.

Second, create a comfortable, inviting atmosphere.

Whether you are at home or traveling, find a comfortable (but not too comfortable) spot for your time alone with God. A window seat, a chair near a fireplace, a lawn chair on a sunny porch, or a favorite nature vista are just a few options for enhancing your experience of being alone with God. (A warm, cozy bed might not be the best place.)

Third, protect your space.

At home, be sure to turn off all electronic devices (telephone, TV, computer) that are designed to get your attention. If you're on an airplane, bring earphones and a music player that will allow you to "tune out" other conversations so that you can concentrate on hearing God talk to you. You might want to play your favorite music to provide an intimate atmosphere for hearing God speak. Eventually, it will become a comfort to you to have a favorite and familiar place for your "God Talks."

Fourth, clear out any hindrances (doubt, sin, poor time management, or lack of interest as discussed in chapter 5).

In addition to clearing off the table, so to speak, by getting rid of the common hindrances to hearing God talk, protect your time with Him by telling others that you have an appointment and you're unavailable during the next hour (or however long) unless there's an emergency. I know that you give this same courtesy to other important meetings; why not do the same for preparing for and carefully protecting your time alone with God? Because urgent interruptions and beautiful or compelling sounds have an incredible power to attract, distract, and hold your attention, I encourage you to take extra measures to artistically create an intimate atmosphere.

The art of hearing God talk—that starts with a discipline and turns into devotion—brings the beauty of a heavenly God into the depths of your individual heart. You validate what you hear God say when you create an atmosphere for intimacy and record your conversations.

Hearing God Talk Takes Patience (the Virtue of Patience)

Patience requires tenacity and perseverance. Patience means waiting. Oh, and *who* likes to wait?

Though it goes without saying, I'm going to say it anyway: Patience, among the many disciplines of a virtuous life, is difficult to master. One of the most prominent authors on the subject of intimacy with God, Oswald Chambers, confessed that "waiting on God is man's greatest stress."[2]

Nonetheless, it is not a matter of opinion that we should acquire the discipline of patience in our conversational relationship with God; it is a fundamental teaching of Jesus:

> One day Jesus told his disciples a story to show that they should always pray and never give up. "There was a judge in a certain city," he said, "who neither feared God nor cared about people. A widow of that city came to him repeatedly, saying, 'Give me justice in this dispute with my enemy.' The judge ignored her for a while, but finally he said to himself, 'I don't fear God or care about people, but this woman is driving me crazy. I'm going to see that she gets justice, because she is wearing me out with her constant requests!' "
>
> Then the Lord said, "Learn a lesson from this unjust judge. Even he rendered a just decision in the end. So don't you think God will surely give justice to his chosen people who cry out to him day and night? Will he keep putting them off? I tell you, he will grant justice to them quickly! But when the Son of Man returns, how many will he find on the earth who have faith?"
>
> LUKE 18:1–8 NLT

R. A. Torrey, in his book *How to Pray*, contended that it is not "submission but spiritual laziness" if you exhibit a lack of willingness to wait, to persevere, or to push through UNTIL you hear God talk to you and give you His answer. He wrote,

> We do not call it submission to the will of God when we give up after one or two efforts to obtain things by action. We call it lack of strength of character. When the strong man or woman of action starts out to accomplish a thing and does not accomplish it the first or second or one-hundredth time,

he or she keeps hammering away until it is accomplished. The strong man of prayer keeps on praying until he prays it through and obtains what he seeks. We should be careful about what we ask from God. But, when we do begin to pray for a thing, we should never give up praying for it until we receive it or until God makes it very clear and very definite that it is not His will to give it.[3]

The psalmist also gives us the perspective that patience is not idle waiting, but a dynamic expectancy that must be nurtured:

> I wait for the Lord, my soul waits,
>   and in his word I put my hope.
> My soul waits for the Lord
>   more than watchmen wait for the morning,
>   more than watchmen wait for the morning.
>
> PSALM 130:5–6

Patience, in fact, is active waiting! Not to oversimplify with this example, but our family dog of fourteen years, Keziah, would patiently wait for us to get out of bed, feed her, walk her, and come home from work and pet her. She would wait at the front door or the kitchen cupboard, or lay by our feet, her eyes watching our every move *until she received what she was waiting for.* She never doubted that we'd take care of her. She knew we loved her. And her waiting proved that she trusted us.

Patient waiting is not passive—it is being watchful, alert, always looking and listening for God to come to you.

Patient waiting expects God to talk to you in *some* way, trusting Him to rescue you.

Patient waiting immediately recognizes and quickly rejects the negative thoughts that steal hope.

Patient waiting refuses to worry, certain that worry only saps your strength.

Patient waiting puts confidence in the truth of God's Word and in His plans for your life, acknowledging His love toward you.

Patient waiting holds on to God's promises, which surpass human understanding and instill just enough comfort and courage *to keep waiting*.

Take your patience to another level and turn it into hope—don't just endure, but expect. Hope always waits and never gives up on hearing God talk.

Hearing God Talk Takes Time (the Management of Time)

If your view of "God Talks" waffles between a good idea that doesn't always produce results, an activity that is primarily performed by those who are assigned to spend time with God (such as clergy—surely not the average man or woman), and an exercise in futility that is inconvenient or boring, now is the perfect *time* to change your perspective.

Many of the classic authors on prayer suggest that you must be diligent—even militant—by jealously guarding your time alone with God. Of course, this assumes you are willing to set aside time for "God Talks" by giving it such importance and priority that it is reflected in a chunk of time on your calendar!

Corrie ten Boom, a Holocaust survivor whose story, *The Hiding Place*, was made into a film by the Billy Graham Evangelistic Association, called her time alone with God "an appointment with the King." In one of her recorded appearances she said, "Don't pray when you feel like it; make an appointment with the King and keep it."

Her thoughts inspire quite a different perspective, don't they? Rather than seeing prayer as a duty you must perform, she encourages you to see yourself entering a throne room and gaining an audience with the most majestic and all-powerful ruler, who amazingly welcomes *you* into His presence at *any time.*

I know you value your time. I, too, consider time my most precious personal commodity. But I submit to you that "God Talks" can be the most exciting appointments of your day; appointments you simply won't want to miss if you change your perspective of them, count the small cost of incorporating them into your daily life, and consider the consequences of missing out on them.

To change your perspective, begin by placing a value on your time alone with God. Here are some of the benefits I've experienced:

- saves time
- reduces stress
- imparts wisdom
- exposes lies
- creates hope
- instills confidence
- eliminates mistakes
- captures eternity

What benefits have *you* experienced when you've set aside time to talk and listen to God?

Next, consider the price you'll have to pay to spend time daily with God. To tell you that making and keeping a daily appointment with God won't cost you something would be dishonest. But you might be surprised at what it has cost me to get alone with God for one hour a day for over twenty-five years. My time with God has *only* cost me a few lunch appointments, a little less sleep, and a little less television. What might it cost you?

Finally, consider the consequences of *not* having a daily appointment with God.

If you skip your daily "God Talks," you might miss hearing . . .

> time-saving instruction,
> > an idea that could save you money,
> > > an insight that would spare you heartache.

More important, I have personally found that if you miss hearing God talk to you—by neglecting to set aside daily time with Him—you'll have less spiritual power in your life. Conversely, by keeping a regular daily appointment with God, more answers will be received and more power will be released in your life than ever before!

Leonard Ravenhill was among many nineteenth- and twentieth-century authors who taught "The men, who prayed most, accomplished most."[4] His predecessor, R. A. Torrey, taught, "We can accomplish more by time and strength put into prayer than we can by putting the same amount of time and strength into anything else."[5]

There was a time when I didn't believe that time alone with God—talking and listening to Him—released more of God's power than physical activity *until I began to spend one hour a day with Him*. After each daily appointment, I would come away with a to-do list that concisely ordered my day into a blueprint for completing tasks and projects. Simultaneously, I found myself repeatedly saying to family and co-workers, "You won't believe what God did today! You won't believe what I heard God tell me to do!" I never wrote a book, never traveled to speak outside of the state I lived in, never filmed a video or spoke at a crusade until I developed the discipline of making and keeping daily appointments with God.

Don't take my word for it. Try it yourself.

Let God Talk to You

Create a Daily Space for Your "God Talks"

Are *you* willing to set a specific amount of time each day to be alone with God? If so, choose a place where you will spend your daily appointment with God. Is it a favorite, comfortable nook or chair in your home; is it by the fireplace, outside on a porch, near water or woods, or at a park? (Take into consideration any drive-time to and from the location, if necessary.)

Second, determine the amount of time you want to spend talking and listening to God: ten or fifteen minutes, thirty or sixty minutes? Then brainstorm the first uninterrupted block of time during the next seven days—note different times for weekday and weekend days. (Your age and responsibilities will usually determine the best time of day on each day of the week for you to meet in an appointment with God—before work or school, during the lunch hour, before bedtime, etc.)

Next, transfer these ideas, placing them on your calendar for the next seven days (similar to any other appointment).

Example: Monday through Friday 7:00 to 7:30 AM
Saturday and Sunday 4:00 to 4:30 PM

Finally, evaluate at the end of seven days how well this system worked for you—and make any adjustments necessary for the next seven days.

Hearing God Talk Takes Practice (the Dedication to Practice)

The practice of *anything* takes discipline. Practice is an outward expression of an inward desire to excel or get better, to become more adept at a skill or to learn *more* about something you already know.

Great athletes, great artists, great inventors, great authors, great actors, or great musicians practice their trade—training their bodies and harnessing their minds—in order to become more skilled, more proficient, and more productive.

Hearing God talk is the same. It is like learning a new language.

Be assured, it takes practice to hear God talk. And as all those in training have experienced, you will inevitably make mistakes when you're learning something new.

There will be times when you misunderstand what God says to you. You will miss opportunities or learn hard lessons because you *flat-out failed* to hear His voice.

But failure, mistakes, hard lessons, and missed opportunities never keep the "greats" from practicing harder, returning to rigorous training, repeating their exercises until they get it right, or recording their forward (and sometimes backward) progress.

In *Hearing God*, Dallas Willard, after two hundred pages of methodical and biblical teaching on how anyone can hear God's voice, admits *there is a learning curve*. He writes, "If I am right, the obedient, listening heart, mature in the things of God, will in such a case find the voice plain and the message clear, as with the experiences of the friends of God recorded in the Bible. This is a claim that must be tested by experience, and anyone willing to meet the conditions and learn from failures as well as successes can put it to the test."[6]

As I mentioned earlier, my husband, a wise spiritual mentor of mine since before our marriage, suggested that I add a disclaimer to my enthusiastic claims that I've heard God talk. His advice has given me greater freedom to share my experiences with hearing God's voice and tempers the way it is received by others. He's encouraged me to say, "This is what I *think* God is saying to me." Or "I *feel* as if God is saying this to me because of what I've read in the Bible, etc." He taught me that it is possible to be wrong, but it doesn't mean that I can never express my thoughts or feelings that occur during my conversations with God. I simply allow room for my humanness and God's holiness to intersect.

Richard Foster, in *Freedom of Simplicity,* suggests that you experiment with avenues that will open you up to hearing God speak. He also suggests that you "discover as many ways as possible to keep God constantly in mind. 'There is nothing new in that,' you may say. 'That practice is very ancient and very orthodox.' Exactly! This desire to practice the presence of God is the secret of all the saints."[7]

Hearing God Talk Requires the Commitment of All Your Senses

One evening at dusk, I pulled into the parking lot at the local grocery store, intending to pick up a few things for dinner. I had just spent the last few minutes alone in the car thinking about something sad while driving home from my office. As I took my keys out of the ignition and jumped out of the car, I looked up. I couldn't help but see the most vivid red sunset, with shades of gold and blue clouds bordering the width of the sky. I stopped and said, "Oh, wow! God, you're right here. You're so visible. Nothing is too much for you. You want my attention. You want me to hear and see you right now. You don't want me to dwell on what is wrong but on those things that are right and true and good."

That conversation with God immediately lifted me out of my little funk.

I took ten more steps and was standing right in front of my dear friend and walking partner, Cindy. I hadn't seen her coming out of the store because I was so captivated by God. When our eyes met, we were only five feet from each other, so I let out a big "I need a hug!"

She responded, "You do? Then let me hug you!" And in the middle of the busy store entrance, we warmly embraced and laughed. (Though we had taken a fitness walk only weeks before, you might have thought we were long lost cousins who hadn't seen each other in years by how excited we were to see each other!)

After we embraced, she followed up on my original request and asked, "Why do you need a hug?"

"Oh," I shrugged my shoulders and continued, "I was feeling a bit down, but when I saw the sky, I really could sense God trying to get my attention."

She looked at the beautiful sky and sighed deeply.

"How are *you*?" I asked my friend, who has been through one of the toughest ordeals a mother could ever experience. And though time has minimized some of her pain, it has not extinguished it. It never will.

As Cindy began to share the specific details of her day, which had forced her, as small things often do, to relive her pain and remember how deeply she hurts inside, her lips trembled and her voice crackled and tears slipped from her eyes.

I began to cry spontaneously.

In that moment, we were oblivious to the passing customers.

It was as if God had allowed me to hear His voice tell me that He is ever-present in our saddest moments—just in time to "tune in" to my dear friend's very real, always lingering sadness.

Our mutual tears released *just a little* of her pain, and she began to laugh. In fact, almost as quickly as we had burst into tears, we burst into laughter. I commented, "Wow! That was quite an unexpected encounter with God and each other, eh?"

God talks to you through whatever means available. He might send a gentle breeze to touch your face or a piercing ray of sunlight to peek through a dark and cloudy sky to catch your glance. God speaks through moments of stillness or someone else's spoken words. He will make himself known to you through tears or laughter, great sadness, and deep satisfaction.

As you develop the disciplines of hearing God talk, make every effort to engage all of your senses. *God wants you to feel Him as much as hear Him*—to get goose bumps and tingling sensations when you hear His voice, to shudder at the sounds and sights of nature, and to gasp in awe of His power, artistry, and intervention.

Let God Talk to You

Room With a View

Chris Tiegreen, author of *Creative Prayer,* writes, "Historically and biblically, communication between God and humanity has usually been a full sensory experience."[8] He suggests an array of artistic resources to help you develop a more "imaginative, emotional, tangible, artistic, and intimate" conversation with God.[9] In his book, he discusses a variety of ways to experience God by involving posture, sight, sound, taste, and movement. His use of color reflects his conviction that "God does not suppress your emotions, and He doesn't ask you to suppress them either."[10]

Try it: Gather any type of colorful utensils—crayons, pens, colored pencils, paint—find a table with a window view, and fill the air with your favorite instrumental music. Then on blank paper, creatively express your love toward God. Instead of expressing yourself to God in words, express yourself to Him through the use of color, design, texture, and space.

God Wants to Spend Time With You

If you want to truly experience a most intimate and very effective prayer life—where your time alone with God makes you never want to leave His presence—then make every effort to create an inviting atmosphere and develop a disciplined system to make your time with God:

(1) *Nonnegotiable.* Make a specific commitment of time to get alone with God every day. No exceptions. Not only when you feel like it or when it's convenient. This is crucial to overcoming any tendency you might have to procrastinate or give in to fatigue. *Choose* to do it in the beginning if your emotions try to talk you out of your commitment. (As a wife and a new mom who also coached and worked in a nonprofit organization, this new time commitment presented quite a shake-up of my daily schedule, so it would have been very easy to quit.) But I'm convinced, after all these years, that the primary reason I've been able to keep my daily one-hour appointment with God is not because I am inherently disciplined, but because I willingly place my

appointment with God on my calendar, *one day in advance, and not always at the same time.* This single secret has helped me—and thousands of others—keep daily, consecutive appointments with God (they've told me so).

(2) *Cleansing.* Set aside time daily for God to expose and cleanse any impure motives and questionable behavior. No exceptions. Confession of sin is not an option if you want to be "on fire for God"—don't run from it. Don't pretend you don't need it. Call sin what it is in your life; otherwise it will hurt you and shame God. Seek holiness and humility until you acquire it. This takes time. (Kneeling prayer is one practical way to achieve a humble-before-God heart, mind, *and body.*)

(3) *Expectant.* People who spend time with God have access to His power. People who don't, don't. Miracles, supernatural intervention, expectation in the face of disappointment, and the courage to never give up are not results of education but of hearing God talk to you, telling you what He will do for you. When you hear God say, "Keep going," especially when it doesn't make sense or when no one else is cheering you on, His voice will give you what you need to persevere and not give up.

(4) *Two-way conversations.* Prayer is not just talking! This suggestion may seem intriguing, but it's not a new or novel idea. I didn't think of prayer as a two-way conversation with God before attending that youth worker's conference. I used to believe that prayer was simply my telling God how I felt and what I needed (or wanted). I was an out-of-balance, unenlightened, self-centered person when it came to intimacy with God. Allow your alone time to be when you daily ask for and receive God's counsel, and long discussions hammer out strategic ideas until final decisions are made under the presence of His Holy Spirit. If you're like I was, this might be quite unfamiliar to you. You might be more prone to releasing quick, urgent requests when all things go haywire. Or perhaps you're more comfortable impulsively barreling through obstacles rather than stopping to consult God first. If so, setting aside time daily to both *talk* and

listen to God will definitely require a conscious change of communication style.

God is not content just knowing you or occasionally attracting your attention; He wants to regularly be with you! From the hundreds of books I've read and from my personal experience over the past twenty-five years, neither desire nor discipline is enough to sustain a consistent or daily appointment with God. You'll also need a *design* that will make letting God talk to you a daily reality.

CHAPTER 8

Have a Daily Design for "God Talks"

In the van on the way home from the conference in Chicago, I told all my co-workers that I had made a lifelong decision to spend one hour a day with God—*and most of them chuckled.* They knew me. They knew just how excited I got about new things *and* just how quickly my exuberance diminished when confronted with the tediousness of hard work. (They had witnessed my numerous previous attempts to succeed at the hottest fad diets—to no avail.)

As passionate as I was in that moment, their skepticism powerfully motivated me to find some practical way to:

> overcome my tendency to be easily distracted,
>
> keep my word to God, *and*
>
> prove them wrong!

Determined but clueless, the first morning back home after the conference, I faced a huge dilemma: "How am I going to do this? I'm not good at this—I never finish a project. I can hardly sit still in a meeting. How am I going to be quiet for an hour?

How am I going to keep a commitment to pray for one hour a day for the rest of my life?"

So I simply asked God for an idea to organize my first hour in prayer. Within minutes a thought followed, which I assumed was from God: *Keep a written record of our conversations.*

I learned a very important lesson that morning: *God talks. He does!*

In any and every moment of frustration or confusion, instead of worrying or fretting or talking about your concerns to others, talk to God *first*. Then listen for His answer.

The first of my more than nine thousand "God Talks" began right then and there at my kitchen table. I wrote down everything I said to Him and recorded everything I felt or heard God say to me. (By the way, I have kept almost every page of our two-way conversations since 1984. Not only do I have a written record of what I've said to God, but how God met me in every situation and answered every concern of my heart—which has included a fair number of no's.)

Praying the Write Way

I attribute my unbroken string of daily appointments with God not to devotion or creativity, inherent discipline or spiritual maturity, but to the simple, daily activity of keeping a written record of our two-way conversations. Writing has been the singular solution to overcoming my previous weaknesses of procrastination and daydreaming. So if you have struggled repeatedly to develop a powerful and consistent prayer life, I am confident you will benefit from keeping a written record of your conversations with God in a prayer journal or notebook.

Just a few benefits of praying the "write way" include:

Focus: With pen and paper, you are forced to be attentive to one subject. You have one focal point. Your conversations don't trail off into outer space when you're writing. You have to finish sentences and make decisions—or not. In other words, when talking to God in writing, you acknowledge that someone is conversing *with* you—this isn't a diary of your day, but a letter of intent. *Writing gets all your senses moving in the same direction.*

Accountability: When you write down what you believe or think or hope for, it takes your thoughts to a new level of commitment. Written words are visible—black on white. The greatest example of this is the Bible—where God's words and promises are made visible to you. He's accountable to you. You, by writing to Him, become accountable for your words and actions. In fact, your personal integrity is on the line. Any disparity between your words and actions becomes clear when you write one thing but do or say the opposite. *You get untangled from your lusts and laziness by making decisions in writing.*

Recall: It's very easy to forget the innumerable details or promises you make to others—unless you write them down. You are not only reminded to bring the needs of others to God because their names are written in your journal or notebook, but you are also reminded of decisions that you made before God days or months earlier. *Written commitments are very hard to ignore and not so easy to forget.*

Action: Written words, like contracts, inspire if not demand commitment. "I will" is different than "I'll try." When written down, "I will" turns an intention or a good idea into a pledge of your money, time, and action. Imagination turns into animation when you write down on paper what is in your mind. I have proof. Without spending one hour daily with God, I obviously wouldn't be writing this book; I might not even be an author. I doubt I would have over thirty years of sobriety—my family tree suggests otherwise. I don't know if I'd be married to the same man for over thirty years—especially when more than half of the couples who got married when we did are now divorced.

And I've been healthy for over twenty-five years. For a former overeater, overdrinker, and pill-popper, that's a good report! *You will become more productive, in every area of your life, if you talk to God—in writing—about your goals and desires.*

A Proven Pattern

Since 1984, I have recorded my "God Talks" by following the same pattern every single day. Those of you who are familiar with me—through books or speaking engagements—have undoubtedly heard me share about the simple idea God gave me to keep my two-way conversations with Him stored in a refillable notebook. *My Partner Prayer Notebook*[1] has ten tabbed sections that for over twenty-five years have kept my two-way conversations with God accountable and organized. The first four tabs are the sections in which *I talk to God* and the next six tabs are the sections in which *God talks to me* during our daily, one-hour appointment.

People often ask me, "How do you fit all these aspects of prayer into one hour?" And I answer, "Believe me, if I didn't have a system to follow, I'd easily spend most of my time requesting, some of my time daydreaming, and none of my time with God, admitting my sins to Him."

So all these years, I've used the same simple but inviting design for recording my conversations with God. In fact, I've taught this system to millions of adults and students at events or through radio and television shows. Most important, since 1984, I've never had any reason to give it up or change it up. My track record—and that of hundreds of thousands of others—proves that it works for the young or old, busy or easily distracted, and especially for the not-so-organized people who desperately want to connect with God on a daily basis!

My Partner Prayer Notebook[2] guides me daily to talk to God by:

- Praising Him,
- Admitting my sins to Him,
- Requesting of Him, and
- Thanking Him.

It gives me a daily place to record the many ways I hear God talk to me through:

- Listening to the Holy Spirit,
- Messages spoken by others,
- New Testament readings,
- Old Testament readings,
- Proverbs readings, and the
- To-do's that come to mind.

Each of these conversational aspects of my "God Talks" serves a purpose. And if I had endless space and time, I could give you twenty-five reasons why *each* of them has been so important in both developing discipline in my life and fanning the flame of my devotion to God. Instead, I'll just give you the very best reasons they have endured the test of time and remain the design for my daily two-way conversations with God.

Talking to God

Talking is easier than listening for most of us. Even so, talking to God can be intimidating unless you follow a pattern that has both order and honor to it. Here is my suggestion:

Begin your "God Talks" with words of *praise* for Him.

Tell God how and why you trust Him, then *admit*—agree—that you need help to change one or more areas of your life.

Next, make specific *requests*—ask God for His immediate and divine intervention for yourself and others.

Finally, *thank* Him for His help—acknowledge how and when and where He has made himself available to you.

Praise God!

There is an unspoken order to any conversational relationship, most especially with God. Early on, I instinctively understood that when you want to daily converse with the King of Kings and Lord of Lords, it is simply more respectful and polite to begin by honoring Him with your words of affirmation than to stampede into the room and blurt out your complaints or unload your list of needs.

So how does an average human being approach and offer praise to the living, loving God?

Imagine entering the highest court, a royal throne room, or the office of a president. Your demeanor is respectful. Your attitude is attentive. Your first words will undoubtedly be full of admiration. Your head might be bowed, or your hands lifted high—this is praise!

Praise sets the tone, or the ambiance, for your conversations with God. Praise positions your heart. Praise is the place of entry and invitation. *(Note: Praising God is not thanking Him for doing something specific—that will come later. This is your chance to praise God for WHO He is. Praise is the time and place to tell God how great you think He is, to profess your faith and confidence in Him.)*

Of course, if you're more casual than formal, you'll appreciate knowing that a guide already exists for praising God. The book of Psalms is a book of "God Talks." It contains 150 recorded two-way conversations between human beings and God. Eugene Peterson, in his preface to the book of Psalms in *The Message* (a paraphrase version of the Bible) wrote, "Most Christians for most of the Christian centuries have learned to pray by praying the Psalms."[3]

Peterson describes prayer not as an advanced language but an elementary one. He writes, "It is the means by which our language becomes honest, true, and personal in response to God. It is the means by which we get everything in our lives out in the open before God."[4]

In 1984, when I first started my hour with God each day in praise, I didn't realize this historical pattern existed. But I quickly discovered the book of Psalms as my personal "praise prayers" when I ran out of ideas on how to praise God in the wee hours of the morning, alone in my kitchen, without a choir leading me in a chorus!

Praising God is the "opener" in your two-way conversation with Him. It is your invitation, asking Him to be real with you, signaling to Him that you are ready to be real with Him. And if you use the psalms as your template for praising God, you continue the legacy of recording your conversations with God for others to read.

Written prayer is not a new idea—but it is a good one!

There are 150 psalms from which to choose. There are numerous long ones and many shorter ones to show you how to praise God. Over time, you will acquire favorite psalms, ones that most resonate with you. And no matter how often you read (or pray) them, you will be amazed at how fresh they seem, how deeply they touch you, or how powerfully they guide you on any given day.

Here's a sampling of a few of my favorite psalms of praise:

Psalm 40:1–3: "I waited patiently for the Lord; he turned to me and heard my cry. He lifted me out of the slimy pit, out of the mud and mire; he set my feet on a rock and gave me a firm place to stand. He put a new song in my mouth, a hymn of praise to our God. Many will see and fear and put their trust in the

Lord." I can't help but think I could have written every word of this psalm, as it so perfectly describes the life of an addict who has been given not only a new life, but an opportunity to help others as well.

Psalm 45:1, 11: "My heart is stirred by a noble theme as I recite my verses for the king; my tongue is the pen of a skillful writer. . . . The king is enthralled by your beauty; honor him, for he is your lord." I've memorized many of the verses in the forty-fifth psalm. As both an author and God's follower, I often see myself as a spokesperson for the Lord. The psalms, this one in particular, continually challenge me to love God with all of my life and all of my words.

Psalm 135:4: "For the Lord has chosen Jacob to be his own, Israel to be his treasured possession." I recall reading this verse on the exact day of my son Jacob's seventeenth birthday. He attended a public school, and though I prayed for him daily, I felt and heard God saying something more important to me. It went something like this:

> Jacob is your only son. You are the only woman in his life right now who will show him how much I love him. There isn't a teacher or girlfriend or another friend's mother who loves him like you do and like I do. Increase your prayers for him. As he leaves for college, increase your fasting for him. Treat him as your most treasured possession.

When Jake came home from high school that afternoon, I told him, "Jake, I got a word from the Lord for you today!" He, like a typical teenager, asked, "Yeah, what was that?" I then gave him the verse and said something way too mushy and spiritual, "You are God's treasured possession and you're my treasured possession." I also mentioned that I felt God had asked me to pray and fast for him weekly throughout the rest of high school and college. He gave me that "look"—the one that says you aren't so sure you want someone to do what they just said they were going to do.

It's been over thirteen years since I read that verse on his birthday. But I'll never forget the day I read it, how I felt when I read it, how it impacted my life and kept me focused on the commitment to be a praying, fasting mother when I didn't always feel like it! In fact, it was almost a decade before I felt God release me from fasting one or more meals each week for my son. Right about that time, he returned home to live with us after years away studying and working. Within a few short months, he met a great gal, and they married a year later. I recall the day I told her about this verse and how I knew the day would come when someone would love him more than me. The day and the person had arrived!

Praise is a willing act of worship that instantly transports you into the presence of a holy God.

Let God Talk to You

Praise

Begin by reading one to five psalms each day, paraphrasing them in your own words. Allow them to reflect your emotions and increase your devotion toward God. The psalms give you courage and confidence to tell God exactly what you are feeling and thinking. They give you permission to call God by many names: Father, Friend, Companion, Savior, Warrior, Creator. The psalms give you a new vocabulary for talking to God; they teach you how to pray. Make them your personal praise prayers!

Admit It!

One of the first and most important conversations you will ever have with God is when you admit to Him that you are a sinner.

But as you grow in your relationship with God, if you're typical, you might begin to avoid the constant admission of sin primarily because it seems as if it shouldn't be a factor in your life anymore. Many fall into the trap of ignoring sin or hiding it.

John Owen, a favorite author of mine, gave me a different perspective of sin in his treatise called *Sin and Temptation*. (His unusual terminology gave both sin and temptation a persona.) He suggested that sin will never, ever stop chasing after you—it continuously, relentlessly fights against God and for you! He was convinced that sin never gives up trying to destroy your life, your relationships, or your witness. It will entice you and try to dominate your thoughts until you succumb to it.

Owen believed the only way to rid yourself of sin is to *hate*, rather than love, that which tempts you. How do you hate something that at one time you loved (and maybe still love a little bit)? John Owen contended that hating and shaming and exposing sin is the secret to getting rid of it for good.[5] Rather than minimizing or rationalizing or calling it a bad habit, call sin what it is in your life: *sin!*

Practically speaking, because it is easier to forgo or forget the need to come clean with God and others, most of us need *something* to remind or prompt us to pursue it.

Perhaps it isn't so surprising that God prompted me—a recovering alcoholic, a previously sexually immoral young woman, someone with a pretty volatile temper and competitive nature—to include *near the very beginning* of my conversations with God a section called **Admit,** where I come clean with Him every single day. God knew that I would need to purposely set aside a time and a place where He and I honestly evaluated and assessed the previous twenty-four hours of my life. Every day when I turn to the **Admit** tab and see a blank page, I hear God ask me, "What has been tempting you? Where are you falling short? Are you returning to old patterns or hiding something from me or from those closest to you?" And every day He waits for me to answer these or similar questions. (This section provides me with a daily "intentional listening" exercise.)

Recently, I've read a number of the classic books written on the subjects of sin and its counterpoint: holiness. In *Real Christianity*, William Wilberforce spoke as if to convince others, saying, "Common to all [believers] is the desire for holiness."[6] With each passing generation since he wrote these words, I think he'd find that holiness is not a captivating concept to believers but considered a rather antiquated idea.

Yet the Bible, in both the Old (Leviticus 11:44) and New Testaments (1 Peter 1:15–16), discusses holiness as a nonnegotiable attribute that God requires of His people.

In a practical sense, holiness is getting clean and right with God on a *daily* basis. Therefore, daily confession of any known sin in your life (big, little, ugly, not so ugly) must become nonnegotiable, especially if you want to experience the benefits of being clean before God:

- healing (James 5:16)
- a powerful and effective prayer life (James 5:16)
- forgiveness (1 John 1:9)
- purifying from all unrighteousness (1 John 1:9)
- usefulness to God, preparedness to do any good work (2 Timothy 2:21)

Without the practice of regular admission of sin, your body, mind, and soul will become dirtier and dirtier, less healthy, less productive, and ultimately less powerful and effective in prayer.

It sounds scarier and more difficult than it is, honestly.

A very similar phenomenon occurs with overeaters (which include a lot of us) who avoid daily accountability through regular weigh-ins. For example, if you are on a diet (food or calorie restriction) but keep eating more food than you should, or the wrong foods, and refuse to weigh in regularly, *hoping* you won't gain weight—you'll still gain weight. Overeating plus *hope* won't make your clothes fit. And ignoring weigh-ins won't change the truth. It only makes things worse. And when you do finally get on the scale, it won't be just two pounds that you've gained, it will be an extra twenty pounds that you've let creep onto your body. Inevitably, you'll be miserable.

Similar to a daily weigh-in for dieters is the **Admit** aspect of your daily conversations with God. It is a personal integrity check-in system. You obviously can omit the confession of sin or ignore that it exists, but that won't change the truth about your life. Admitting your sins to God *daily* will keep your interior life honest and clean before God.

In this section, record—in writing—the date and time of your confession, then identify specific offenses, expressing your remorse and regrets, as well as specific action steps you're willing to take toward restitution or to make amends. (I accidently left my notebook on the counter of a local stationery store—you can imagine how quickly I made a U-turn when I realized my sins were sitting on the counter for everyone to read!)

The pattern I've followed is to begin this section of my notebook by writing out two verses from Psalm 139 (vv. 23–24 NLT):

> Search me, O God, and know my heart;
>> test me and know my anxious thoughts.
> Point out anything in me that offends you,
>> and lead me along the path of everlasting life.

These words ask God to shine a light on your darkness, to reveal your lousy, irrational, selfish motives. They open up your inner life to God. They let your guard down, especially when your guard doesn't want to come down! And as quickly as you let God in, He immediately shows you why what you've been doing (or holding on to) isn't going to help your situation, much less improve your relationships or reputation. He purposefully exposes the lies you believe. He instills you with courage to clean up your act. He gives you practical, not magical, suggestions for resolution and restitution. Then He expectantly waits for you to respond to His ideas.

In each of my books, I've divulged how this section of my "God Talks" has included my personal confessions—ranging from angry outbursts toward my son when he was still a toddler to uncontrolled anger I have exhibited within professional relationships. Not so pretty. My husband finally suggested that I should get an "anger sobriety chip," just like the chips I've received for my thirty-plus years of alcohol sobriety.

I'll never forget the day I was on the phone with an airline agent and my voice kept getting louder and sounding more frustrated. From the back of the house, I heard my husband call out to me, asking, "Hey . . . is somebody losing their 'chip' in there?" I immediately stopped myself. My cheeks turned red, and I apologized to the airline agent for raising my voice, telling her I was on the brink of losing my "anger sobriety chip." She kindly forgave me and offered to speak to my husband if it would help me keep my "chip."

We've all seen it. We've all been shocked to know someone whose life and words presented one picture, but it fell completely apart when some hidden or unconfessed sin was made public.

Take the **Admit** aspect of your daily conversation with God seriously. Don't let little habits get overlooked, such as lustful thoughts and glances. Don't allow judgmental attitudes, lack of self-control, or unrighteous prejudices to flitter in and out of your heart, mind, or mouth without regularly dealing with them.

Let God Talk to You

A "Confession Session"

Open the Bible to Psalm 139:23–24, and make this your prayer. Along with writing down these verses, record any thoughts God brings to your mind—such as unforgiveness or bitterness or anger toward someone. Then ask God to give you courage to let go of your woundedness or pride. Ask Him to forgive you and give you strength to forgive others.

Allow yourself to have a back-and-forth discussion with God in the **Admit** section of your notebook. Tell Him your struggles. Speak truthfully—if you're being whiny or selfish, you'll probably notice it before God says anything! Let God know what is frustrating to you and why. Then let Him speak back to you— giving you suggestions. For example, He might tell you how to specifically make amends with someone you've hurt. He might give you closure in a different, more personal way, than you could ever conceive on your own. God might ask you to make restitution that could cost you money—and He'll even give you ideas for payment plans. He might ask you to immediately remove something from your home or your vocabulary. And He'll always give you an opportunity to respond to His suggestions. If He suggests that you get outside help—see a pastoral counselor or join a small accountability group for a specific problem—don't hesitate to do what He says. Quick, humbling resolve and restitution is much less painful than ongoing public humiliation.

Of course, not every day will include an enormous confession of sin. But on those occasions when you have truly erred— hurting God, yourself, and/or others—and you're struggling to find your way back to a clean heart and right spirit, please, don't leave this section without hearing God talk to you. Allow Him to restore your soul. (This is another reason for hour-long appointments with God—you feel less rushed and more willing to stay with Him if you've already set aside ample time to talk with Him each day.)

Restoration is an emotional, physical, and spiritual experience with God. The more transparent you are with Him and the more often you sincerely admit your sins to Him, the more quickly you will recognize His releasing you from guilt and shame (1 John 1:9). You'll almost feel something lift off and move away from you. Stay with God—don't leave Him—until it lifts.

Honestly, there will be many more days during your confession session when you are merely continuing a discussion with God regarding a recurring area in which you are tempted to slip back into an old habit, but have not yet done so. Acknowledge this tension, don't minimize it. Get comfortable with the balance between proactively fending off temptation and immediately admitting to God any known sin in your life. The more often you do this, the easier it becomes.

And on those rare days when you're fortunate enough not to be hampered by pesky temptations or bogged down with an extended time of confession—and you're actually enjoying momentary progress—make it a point to humbly admit your continuous, never-ending need for God to keep you strong and safe, alert to temptation or pride.

Though I didn't consciously design an order to my conversations with God, He did.

I didn't realize until years after I had been following the Praise-Admit-Request-Thanks pattern that requests of God are best made from a confident, bold, and clean heart. Therefore, when talking to God, your **Request** prayers should strategically follow the **Admit** section of your prayer time, or in your prayer notebook. This assures you that you will have more power in prayer (James 5:16). (That would be the goal, right?)

In addition to many other Bible verses, the following verses from the book of Psalms confirm this integral connection between a clean heart before God and the release of God's power in prayer:

> *Psalm 66:18:* "If I had cherished sin in my heart, the Lord would not have listened."

> *Psalm 84:11:* "No good thing does he withhold from those whose walk is blameless."

Coming to God with a pure heart and clean mind gives you confidence to talk to Him about the needs of others, while simultaneously giving you boldness to talk to others about Him.

Admission of sin is a willing act of humility that instantly transports you into the presence of a holy God.

Request It!

Why do so few people set aside time daily to pray for themselves or others? Requesting prayer is time-intensive. I've heard the complaints: asking, requesting, and interceding prayer is boring and repetitive.

Over the past twenty-five years, I've never gotten tired of praying for people because there is always a reward: changed lives, healing, restoration, salvation, and lots more answers! Author and theologian O. Hallesby taught what all praying people eventually find true in their own prayer lives: "When God grants our prayers, it is because He loves us; and when He does not, it is because He loves us."[7]

A **Request** list or section in a prayer notebook can certainly become tedious—*if you let it*—because it requires focus and intention. It *is* work, in a very literal sense. Rather than seeing your request list as ideas or hopes being wistfully tossed into the air, you must see yourself *approaching God* with the needs of yourself and others. In His presence, you can actually lift up or bring forward the names and needs of those who are sick, making specific requests on their behalf. By diligently and daily bringing those you know and love to God's attention—asking that their plans go smoothly, for them to be safe and healthy, for their finances and families to be protected—you are not wasting time, but giving a gift of your time spent on their behalf.

A prayer **Request** list is neither a wish list nor a tell-God-what-to-do list. Requesting prayer is an experience with God where you ask, then watch and wait for Him to answer. Renowned preacher Charles Spurgeon pushed people to regularly ask of God in prayer, asserting, "Whether we like it or not, asking is the rule of the kingdom."[8]

In addition to the verses in the New Testament books of Matthew (7:7–8) and Luke (11:1–13) where Jesus teaches His disciples and followers to ask, ask, and keep asking, Philippians 4:6 gives another perspective for asking God: "Do not be anxious about anything, but in everything, by prayer and petition, with thanksgiving, present your requests to God." Don't worry; instead ask. Don't demand; instead ask. Don't assume; instead ask.

The greatest reason you and I should be thrilled to spend time daily with God, asking Him about everything, is because He has the answers and the power. We don't!

After twenty-five years, I've received some of the greatest and most exciting answers to prayer as well as experienced some of the most disappointing moments when God did not answer my requests in the manner I had asked or hoped. But I have never felt abandoned by God—I have learned to trust what I can't see and what I know is true: God has a plan. God loves me. He has the power and the ability to change anything at any time. I am better off waiting than fretting. I don't know the future, but I know that He is trustworthy. I stay close to Him, even in my disappointments.

I can honestly say that those discouraging times have not deterred me from continually bringing my numerous requests to God in daily prayer. In fact, the sum of my experience has overwhelmingly fueled my faith to talk to God *more* often, to ask *more* boldly of Him, believe *more* passionately in Him, and pray *more* specifically.

I doubt any individual could convince you that God wants, even waits, for you to ask Him to do something specific, powerful, or impossible. That is because requesting prayer is a personal experience between you and God. Your faith and trust in Him is tested when you ask something specific and then wait to see how He will answer you.

Therefore, I encourage you to experiment with asking prayers. Here is a framework for developing your own **Request** list:

Ask Specifically

Charles Stanley, a contemporary pastor and author, believes you miss out on many answers to prayer if you don't pray specifically.

I've met people who actually take offense at the idea of asking God for specific things. These people consider someone a nuisance who asks God to answer a specific prayer. They believe He is too busy caring for either the sick or "important" people to have time to attend to the "unimportant" needs of average people. Mistakenly, they think they're being too selfish if they ask for something for themselves, such as a price to be lowered on a property in order that they might be able to afford it, or for a loved one to receive a physical healing, or to be hired for a job they really want. Before making a judgment on asking specifically, I suggest that you look up every verse in the Bible that contains the words *ask, believe,* or *pray.* Don't base something as important as your prayer life on what others say—including me!

For example, when I dug into the Bible and discovered exactly what God says about prayer, I realized how much excitement and adventure and power I was missing.

One of the eye-opening verses that changed my perspective of requesting prayer is found in James 4:2–3: "You do not have, because you do not ask God. When you ask, you do not receive, because you ask with wrong motives." This verse doesn't scold you by saying that you should not ask God. Instead, it suggests that you don't have what you want *because you don't ask God*! Asking God specifically for something, of course, will increase or decrease your chances of receiving what you ask for. Perhaps that is the real reason many of us refuse to pray specifically—we don't want to be disappointed, we don't want to look foolish, and we don't want to deeply consider our own motives for asking.

In addition to the numerous examples of requesting prayers (Abraham, Moses, Nehemiah, Gideon, David, and Daniel) found in the Bible, research for yourself what Jesus taught about prayer. He both taught and modeled *how to pray* to all who followed Him. Not only did He give a practical template in what is called The Lord's Prayer (Matthew 6:9–14), but Jesus continually asked His heavenly Father to attend to His requests with specific answers: Water was turned into wine, the dead came back to life, the sick were healed, and thousands of hungry people were fed from just a few loaves of bread.

In teaching about prayer, Jesus did not suggest that you hold back your requests. In fact, He taught that you should not be afraid to ask God for anything. Jesus said, "Ask and it will be given to you; seek and you will find; knock and the door will be opened to you. For everyone who asks receives; he who seeks finds; and to him who knocks, the door will be opened" (Matthew 7:7–8).

Jesus' words inspire me. I've tested His words and found that He says what He means: "Ask." Don't just wish or wait or wonder how or what to pray. I encourage you to ask God specifically for what you need. This section will become very exciting to you when you ask specifically, because you will get some specific answers. For the record, you must be as willing to accept a "no" answer as often and as graciously as you accept "yes" answers in response to your requests.

Ask Immediately

I've been heavily influenced by the teachings and lives of D. L. Moody, Charles Finney, and Charles Spurgeon—great evangelists from the nineteenth century. In fact, I've read many of their books numerous times, and each time I have walked away with the impression that they attributed the potency behind their powerful preaching to the importance and priority they placed on their personal prayer lives. They were each adamant that a leader's personal time alone with God is the only explanation for any outward success in ministry.

In Charles Finney's *Lectures on Revival*, he disclosed a simple prayer that he believed *always* released a noticeable, supernatural power of God upon a person or in a room when it was uttered:

> "Lord, I pray for an immediate outpouring of your Holy Spirit. . . ."

Since the first day I read of his confidence in this prayer, I began to pray the same prayer each time I would personally pray for an individual or open or close a lecture. I am not suggesting that this is a magic formula, but if you believe God willingly responds to your requests, it is a prayer that will change the boldness with which you ask God when you pray.

When you ask God for His *immediate* outpouring, His *immediate* presence, and His *immediate* power to be released within a situation, you are asking God to do something NOW—before you leave each other, before you finish praying, before the day is over. You can even ask Him to immediately touch the lives of those who are not present.

An attitude of immediacy in prayer brings God into the moment, into your presence. You are being bold and expectant. You have asked Him to pour out His Holy Spirit, and unless you don't mean it or don't believe He will do just that, you can expect Him to do so.

When I pray this prayer, I expect God to pour His Holy Spirit immediately all over me and those for whom I pray, and He does. Here are just a few of the ways I recall God working through this particular prayer request:

> I've opened a meeting with this prayer, and after sharing my testimony, at least three times that I know of, an entire student athletic team gave their lives to Christ. (That never happened before I prayed this prayer.)

> I've prayed this prayer with at least two persons who afterward told me they had intended to commit suicide that very night. At the end of our prayer, because they changed their minds, I was able to direct them to people who could help them further.

> I've prayed this prayer with young women who for months could not stop doing what they were doing. After this prayer, we continued to stay in touch, and they remained free from temptation for many months, some for over a year now.

> I've prayed this prayer with three different young men who were shaking so badly from the humiliation of their confession that they could not stop. At the end of this simple prayer, they abruptly stopped crying and shaking, and then sighed deeply. We immediately knew only God could have given them that release of peace.

> I've prayed this prayer in a room full of Christian business-persons who were expecting a sales talk, but before my presentation was over, an older gentleman not only cried in front of his peers, but confessed his sin, unsolicited.

I pray this prayer ALL THE TIME NOW. Asking God to immediately release the outpouring of His Holy Spirit has changed me. And it has changed others. Most important, I believe God wants to answer this prayer!

Ask Confidently

George Müller was called the "believing pray-er" by many because he taught—throughout his lifetime—that there is a certain connection between believing in the impossible and asking for it. In fact, Müller felt that if you did not have confidence to pray for something, perhaps it was because God had not given you the faith that He would answer that particular prayer. He would even ask people *not* to pray for a certain request if they showed any doubt that God was able to answer it.

Of course, of all persons who consistently saw God do miraculous things—such as move a dense fog so the ship he was on could get from England to Canada in time for him to preach, or bring enough food to an orphanage door at dinnertime to feed children who otherwise would have no food that evening, or provide the exact amount of money to pay a bill within hours before it was due—George Müller stands out as one who often asked of God confidently, and repeatedly saw Him do the impossible.

Müller also believed you could not muster up enough faith on your own to pray. You should instead ask God to give you confidence and courage to pray in a specific way, and then pray in that manner.

The author of Hebrews (4:16) said it this way: "Let us then approach the throne of grace with confidence, so that we may receive mercy and find grace to help us in our time of need."

Your confidence in making requests of God cannot be focused on your own power or ability, but in God's. Constantly remind yourself to whom you are praying: the One who is able to do immeasurably more than all you could ask or imagine (Ephesians 3:20). Therefore, if He gives you the confidence that He is going to do something for you or for someone else, pray believing that He will do as He said He would do. (*Note:* You don't have to tell others what or how God has instructed you to pray; that is between Him and you.)

Ask Scripturally

If you don't know where to begin or if you lack confidence in how to talk to God, a wonderful way to learn to pray—especially, but not only, if you are a parent—is through a guide compiled by Jodie Berndt called *Praying the Scriptures for Your Children*. It's a resource filled with Scripture verses from the entire Bible that have been researched and chosen for you (the hard work has been done), helping you to know how to pray. All you have to do is choose a chapter that relates to the age or season of your child's life—from birth through the school years, sports, friendships, and marriage—and insert her name in the blank.

For example, I only began to use this resource after my son left for college. In fact, I photocopied a few of the pages from chapters titled "Praying for Your Child's Purpose in Life"; "When He or She Leaves Your Nest"; and "Praying for Your Child's Marriage."

For many years, I carried about eight pages of Scripture prayers in the pockets of my prayer notebook until they were worn and tattered. I inserted my son's name in scenarios based on such verses as Genesis 29:20: "Cause _____ to be willing to wait for your perfect timing in finding a [spouse], even as Jacob waited seven years to marry his beloved Rachel."[9]

One night, while out for coffee with some college students from my church, two young girls at the end of the table mentioned they were soccer players. My ears (and my radar) perked up! I thought, *Oh, soccer-playing, churchgoing college students would be great friends for my son!*

So I threw out a suggestion: "Hey, if you need an extra soccer player for the local coed games, my son would probably join you on a moment's notice! I could give you his cell number, and you could send him a text message the next time you need a substitute." The girls took his number. The very next Friday, Jake got a text message inviting him to play on their team and he did. The following week, he was invited to play soccer with them again—and because it was Easter weekend, they all attended church together as well. I was delighted—my son hadn't been to church that many times in the previous month let alone in one weekend. He went once each on Thursday, Friday, and Saturday, and twice on Sunday!

Each day after that Easter Sunday and for many months to follow, Jake spent time with one of the young women—the cute, soccer-playing nursing student named Khara.

At the end of the summer, my son asked his dad and me if he could invite Khara to join us for the Italian family reunion that was being held at a campground in Ohio. We knew this would be an important indicator of their future. So on the morning my son left early to golf with his many aunts and uncles, I invited Khara to join me at the poolside where I would be spending my hour with God. She came along, and after about thirty minutes into our quiet times, I pulled out my "Scriptures for Jake." My hands were shaking as I realized that the future wife of my son, whom I had been praying for daily for well over two decades—could be sitting next to me! I also realized that she hadn't even been born yet when I began to pray for my son's wife.

I had been praying the following Scriptures:

"You know the plans you have for *Jake*. . . ." (Jeremiah 29:11–13)

"Fulfill every good purpose in *Jake's* life. . . ." (2 Thessalonians 1:11–12)

"No matter what are the plans in *Jake's* heart, let your purpose prevail in his life." (Proverbs 19:21)

Spontaneously, I looked over to the lawn chair next to me and asked Khara if she would like to see how I prayed for my son. As she took the tattered pages from my hand, you could almost feel a spiritual and emotional connection occur between us. She quietly read the verses and smiled, then handed them back to me without speaking. I think we were both too choked up to speak to each other.

At the campground, Jake and Khara played as a team in every competitive sport possible. For every reason, Khara was a perfect fit for my son and his big Italian Tirabassi family, but most especially because she loved God, had a passion to play sports, and wanted, like my son, to dedicate her life to mission work.

The following Thanksgiving, Jake and Khara came to us and asked if they could get married on Easter weekend on a beach (of course)! They especially wanted all visiting family and friends to join us for Easter services the day after their wedding. How could we say no?

A few months after the wedding, I found a thank-you card from my new daughter-in-law tucked away in my purse after I dropped the newlyweds off at the airport. I couldn't help but see the payoff of twenty-plus years of praying for the wife of my only son. It read (of course I've saved it):

> You are so supportive of our marriage. It means so much to us and we just want you to know that you are appreciated. Thank you especially for your prayers, we don't thank you enough for those. Love, *Jake and Khara*

You don't have to have children to pray Scriptures for yourself or others. Find appropriate verses in the Bible as templates for (1) releasing powerful prayers on behalf of those you love; (2) articulating your need for God's help in difficult situations; and (3) building your faith so that you will grow closer to God. For example, Habakkuk 3:2 is an amazingly powerful Scripture to pray for anyone on any occasion: "I have heard all about you, Lord. I am filled with awe by your amazing works. In this time of our deep need, help us again as you did in years gone by" (NLT).

Ask Persistently

Diligence, tenacity, and perseverance are the nonnegotiable traits of a powerful and effective pray-er. It is not an option to give up praying for someone if God gives you the conviction that you must continue to pray for him or her.

Praying for someone to be healed, to find their soul mate, to get a job, to be freed from emotional oppression, or to be released from an addiction will take time. Consistent prayer, in addition to medical help or pastoral counsel, a healthier diet, or the removal from unhealthy, unholy activities will change a situation.

Neglecting to pray can hinder or stall the release of God's power upon a person's life.

For example, does someone you know need healing? What I've read and personally experienced regarding physical or emotional healing confirms that in most cases, healing is not instantaneous but occurs over time. My readings have included numerous books by Francis MacNutt, a former priest who for decades has seen people healed through prayer and the teaching of the principles of healing prayer. MacNutt and other experts on healing prayer say that healing rarely occurs as a result of a sensational healing experience. And though spontaneous and miraculous healings do happen and have been confirmed, most often healing occurs over time—a few hours, a few days, a few months, or even after a few years.

The rule of thumb is this: Don't stop praying for people to be healed, or saved, or helped, or empowered, or delivered. That is why a prayer request list is so helpful and handy.

Praying daily for people takes time and organization. It is so easy to tell someone you will pray for them, and then completely forget to do so. It can get boring to pray for the same people and the same needs every single day *unless* you believe that every single prayer that you pray is making a difference in their lives.

In his book *Life Together,* Dietrich Bonhoeffer wrote,

Intercession is not general and vague but very concrete; a matter of definite persons and definite difficulties and therefore of definite petitions. The more definite my intercession becomes, the more promising it is. Finally, we can also no longer escape the realization that the ministry of intercession requires time of every Christian.[10]

Persistence in prayer, he believed, is not a matter of intellect or spirituality. It is a practical matter, a sacrifice of time—which anyone can give to God and on behalf of others!

Wesley Duewel also believed that intensity in prayer was integral to seeing more power released in answers to prayer. He wrote in his passionate book *Mighty Prevailing Prayer:* "Instead of giving up, we move into ever more determined intercession until we prevail."[11] Of course, he admits that "prevailing prayer is holy work, fervent labor."[12] Duewel actually pleaded for more people to become mighty, prevailing, persistent, persevering pray-ers, blaming the powerlessness of the church on its lack of praying men and women. He wrote, "God's cause creeps forward timidly and slowly when there are more organizers than agonizers, more workers than prevailing prayer warriors." He challenged his readers: "We need prayer warriors who pray as though God is God and as though Satan is Satan."[13]

If you want the **Request** section of your "God Talks" to have more power and focus, ask:

> specifically,
> > immediately,
> > > confidently,
> > > > scripturally, and
> > > > > persistently.

Requests are a willing act of surrender that instantly transports you into the presence of a holy God.

Let God Talk to You

Requests

This section will be both FUN and WORK!

By developing a prayer list, you have a visible reminder to pray for those you might forget to pray for, as well as to persevere in prayer for those whose lives need more concerted intercession. A prayer request list is not a wish list but a written record of how God is working in your life and others' lives. And it's very exciting when God does the impossible! Finally, a prayer request list allows you to stay fervent in prayer, persistent in prayer, and focused in prayer.

Make a **Request** list that includes your specific needs as well as the needs and concerns of:

> family,
> friends,
> leaders,
> neighbors,
> those who need healing, and
> those who don't know God.

Make sure you leave room under each name for additional needs that come up. Every month or every quarter, refresh your **Request** list by updating prayers that have been answered, adding new names (such as friends of your children), and any other person or concern that is important to you.

Thank God!

Write a thank-you note to God each day, expressing your gratitude to Him for what He has done for you.

This section of your "God Talks" should be exciting. It is the time and place to reflect on how often, how specifically, and how intimately God has answered your prayers—and to thank Him for doing so. It can be as brief as one or two sentences or as long as one or two paragraphs. But expect that on those days when a long-awaited prayer request has been answered, you'll gush endlessly with "woo-hoos!" and "wows!"

Make it a practice, day after day—even, and especially, on days when you are hurting—to thank God for what He is doing (and has done) in your life. If you thank God on both high and low days, I'm confident that identifying specific answers to your prayer requests will become one of the most enjoyable aspects of your two-way conversations with God! Among its many benefits, not only will your love toward God grow, but you'll become a more appreciative and less selfish person. (Speaking from experience, this is a very practical way to mature in your relationship with God and with others.)

A thank-you note to God looks and feels just the same as a thank-you note to anyone. Just make it personal. Whether you are formal or informal, whether you use bullet points or sentences, daily make it a habit to acknowledge that the Lord of Lords and King of Kings has impacted, influenced, and blessed your life. And be specific.

Do you have a place to live?
Do you have food to eat?
Do you have a spouse who loves you and is faithful to you?
Do you have a great church?
Do you have your health?
Do you have family members or friends who care about you?

Thank God for those things you *do* have, because many people do not have a place to live, food, close friends or family who live near them, a church home, health, or people who love them.

Have you experienced emotional or physical healing?
Have you found something you thought was lost?
Have you been given an opportunity you didn't deserve?

Have you received a call or letter for which you've been waiting?

Have you been surprised by a neighbor's kind gesture or words?

Have you prayed for healing in a relationship and it happened?

Thank God, for many have not experienced healing, joy, opportunity, rescue, kindness, or restoration.

Giving thanks is a willing act of gratitude that instantly transports you into the presence of a holy God.

Let God Talk to You

Your P.A.R.T.

You can also cover these four sections in an abbreviated format: In two minutes each: **Praise** God, using a psalm. **Admit** the most recent sin (anger toward a co-worker, not telling the truth, etc.) you committed, and write it down—use abbreviations if necessary. Begin a **Request** list of the five closest people to you. And write a one-paragraph note of **Thanks** to God for something small, or great!

Listen Up!

At this juncture in your "God Talks," you should begin to talk less and listen intentionally to God talking to you, giving you His thoughts, ideas, and directions.

- Talking to God is where you ask questions.
  Listening to God is where you receive the answers.
- Talking to God expresses your true intentions and motives.
  Listening to God purifies them.
- Talking to God is easy for some.
  Listening to God is hard for most.

- Talking to God invites His presence into your life.
  Listening to God surprises you with His love.

After you spend time talking to God through words of praise, admission, requests, and thanks, continue your two-way conversation with Him by expectantly listening for Him to talk to you through your regular, daily, planned Bible reading; the messages given by your pastoral leaders and spiritual directors; and through the impressions given you by His Holy Spirit. (In chapter 3, I discussed in detail how God talks to you through the Bible, His Holy Spirit, and through the messages of others.)

Theophan the Recluse, a nineteenth-century Russian mystic, wrote,

> When you pray, do not end your prayer without having aroused in your heart some feelings toward God, whether it be reverence or devotion, or thanksgiving, or glorification, or humility and contrition, or hope and trust. Also when after prayer you begin to read, do not finish reading without having felt in your heart the truth of what you have read. These two feelings—the one inspired by prayer, the other by reading [or listening]—mutually warm one another; and if you pay attention to yourself they will keep you under their influence during the whole day. Take pains to practice these two methods exactly and you will see for yourself what will happen.[14]

Listening

Almost like turning the page to welcome a new chapter in a book, when I turn the tab and enter the designated **Listening** section in *My Partner Prayer Notebook,* I stop talking. I place the date on top of a fresh page, and then wait quietly for God to speak to me. Then I write down any key insights I receive, as well as words of affirmation or Scripture verses that come to mind at that moment.

The majority of this book has been dedicated to showing you to whom God talks, as well as how, why, when, and what

God says when He talks. As you develop a daily format for your own "God Talks," consider incorporating the following ideas I have found to be both practical and helpful for capturing God's thoughts and words to me on a daily basis.

Consciously move from talking to God to listening to Him by writing down key insights you receive in a designated **Listening** section of your notebook or journal. These thoughts will often sound parental and loving. Most often, you will hear Scripture— ones that you've memorized or recently heard or read during this time. Write them down. This is one way to let God talk to you. Allow this record to serve as additional confirmation and encouragement of the other thoughts and impressions God has been giving you during the previous hour or day.

Messages

The next tab in *My Partner Prayer Notebook* is titled **Messages**. God regularly wants to talk to you and me through the **Messages**

Let God Talk to You

A Letter Over Time

Test: Begin with a blank sheet of paper—ruled or unlined. Date, then title the page with a specific name, project, or concern. Over a period of four to six weeks, write down—once or many times each day—the words you hear God saying to you. Record the verses you read in your regular daily Bible reading, or verses you hear during sermons or Bible studies, as well as any thoughts or ideas that relate to this concern or that pop into your mind in random conversations or devotional reading.

When you set aside a place—whether in an organized, tabbed note-book or on a blank-paged journal—to record both the serendipitous and consistent ways that God talks to you regarding one issue, you will be amazed at the pattern that unfolds as He directs you toward and confirms His plans.

given during church sermons and Bible studies, or while reading from daily devotional books. As you emotionally or spiritually connect with a specific verse or point, extract the nuggets and record them in an assigned **Message** section of your notebook or journal, so you'll be able to retrieve them when you need them. I actually take my notebook to church each week and take notes during the sermon. By making an outline, recording verses used during the sermon, and even noting choruses that struck a chord with me, I begin to sense the way God is personalizing each message for me.

During the week, I use a favorite short devotional reading as my teacher or messenger. Of course, I've learned that the more challenging the author, the more thought-provoking and life-changing the experience. I keep the message notes for up to a month in my notebook before replacing them with blank refill pages. Month by month, year after year, I collect all my journal pages in a box for occasional review. In essence, since 1984, my recorded two-way conversations with God have not only chronicled a running dialogue of my time with God and others, but they have chronicled my life.

Bible Reading

Next, I continue letting God talk to me through my daily Bible reading—which always includes passages from the **New and Old Testaments, Psalms,** and **Proverbs.** I strongly encourage you to yearly read through a Bible that is divided into 365 daily readings, such as the *Change Your Life Daily Bible.*[15] Its organization will not only allow you to hear God's voice on a day-to-day basis, but it will give you a more complete perspective of who God is and how He communicates to men and women.

Read the Word of God as if God is talking to you—teaching, correcting, directing, or motivating you—whether you are observing the lives of others or sensing His immediate direction in your life. Each day as you study the Word, there is the potential for fresh inspiration, innovative ideas, reminders of a prior commitment you made to God or someone else, conviction of something you should not allow in your life, or encouragement to hold on just a little longer. Like a daily conversation with someone you love, the topics are varied and the action steps are always there for the taking.

I'm convinced that the better you know what the Bible says—not *what others have told you it says or what you think it says*—the more often and easily you'll recognize God's voice when He talks to you.

Let God Talk to You

Identify and Observe

As often as you read the Bible or listen to sermons, I encourage you to regularly identify metaphors and/or observe themes that unfold as you are reading or listening.

What outline or themes do you identify or observe from the parable of the sower found in Luke 8:11–15? (See my observations below to give you an idea of how I apply Jesus' teaching to my life.)

This is the meaning of the parable: The seed is the word of God. Those along the path are the ones who hear, and then the devil comes and takes away the word from their hearts, so that they may not believe and be saved. Those on the rock are the ones who receive the word with joy when they hear it, but they have no root. They believe for a while, but in the time of testing they fall away. The seed that fell among thorns stands for those who hear, but as they go on their way they are choked by life's worries, riches and pleasures, and they do not mature. But the seed on good soil stands for those with a noble and good heart, who hear the word, retain it, and by persevering produce a crop.

Jesus' teaching in Luke 8:4–15 is especially encouraging to me—someone who is extremely passionate about daily Bible reading. Jesus gives His take on the importance of letting the Word of God talk to you. He points out that breezing through the Word won't produce the benefits that retaining it *through perseverance* will provide. I find the teaching very relevant and current to today.

If you read the Word and hold on to it:
> You'll be very productive.
> You won't listen to the devil's lies.
> You won't fall away after testing.
> You won't be choked by life's pressures, treasures, and pleasures.

Take any favorite verse, passage, parable, or teaching and regularly do the same thing: *identify metaphors and/or observe a theme*. Better yet, follow this simple idea daily to gain more insight into your regular, planned Bible reading.

To-Do's

In addition to following a two-way pattern of talking and listening to God through these nine tabbed sections of *My Partner Prayer Notebook*, there is one final section in which I let God talk to me. In a very informal but important **To-Do** section, I jot down any ideas that God gives me during my hourly appointment with Him each day. I have found that if I write down the most insignificant thoughts or random ideas that pop into my mind at any time during my "God Talks," I will undoubtedly save money or time, or even my own reputation, during the next day or week.

The secret of the **To-Do** section is that it's the place to record an idea or task that needs to be accomplished *later*. Whether it is a large or small **To-Do**, transferring the idea in your head to a notepad or calendar (1) acknowledges that you and God have discussed it, and (2) it doesn't actually interrupt your time with God as it would if you physically got up to do it. It simply reminds you to do it *later*!

"God Talks" Are Tangible and Relational

Recording in writing everything you hear, think, and feel God is saying to you makes your two-way conversations with Him tangible and relational rather than mystical or unintelligible. And for those who might need a little convincing that God desires to talk to you every day about everything, keeping a written record of your conversations with Him provides proof that He intimately and practically wants to be involved in your life as well as use you to powerfully change the lives of others.

You may never know why a meeting you were looking forward to attending is cancelled or why you were bumped out of a seat and moved to a later flight. You may never know why God prompts you to decline an invitation, answer an unsolicited call, or accept an offer, especially when it requires sacrifice of your time or money. But if you let God talk to you day after day, becoming very familiar with His voice and willingly responding to His every small (seemingly unimportant) suggestion, you will be ready and alert when He asks you to do something so important that it will significantly impact someone else's life.

You Don't Want to Miss Your Daily "God Talks"

In January 2005, my husband, Roger, was diagnosed with prostate cancer. It was caught early through a random blood test required by an insurance company. After a biopsy, repeated blood tests, much laying-on-of-hands prayer by the elders of our church, and considerable research, we determined to follow a watch-and-wait protocol, which is common for many men with prostate cancer but who maintain a low PSA (Prostate Specific Antigen) count. Additionally, Roger followed a very strict diet, which eliminated white sugar and white flour. His monthly PSA blood tests remained in check, always fluctuating between a very low three and six PSA. Though a PSA count serves as one indicator that the cancer is not spreading, it is not the only indicator. As we prayed daily for a complete and miraculous healing, after much research and medical counsel, Roger became more open to taking a surgical route to remove his cancer if the PSA count ever went above the number six. It was, in essence, a specific prayer request through which we felt God would give us guidance.

One entire page of my **Request** section was dedicated to Roger—his emotional and physical health and his cancer-fighting protocol. Daily, I would discuss my husband's health with God *somewhere, somehow* in each section of my notebook. I spent much time listening to God as well as asking Him to show us when and how to do something different than what we were already doing. Regularly, I would record my fears and concerns, anxieties and sadness, thanks for that month's low PSA count, as well as record God's thoughts to me. My husband did the same thing, and we regularly discussed our God-impressions with each other.

In the summer of 2006, I spoke at a large convention in Estes Park, Colorado. After a general session, I conducted a small workshop on "God Talks" for women. In the workshop, I felt more comfortable sharing Roger's very personal health problem because my lecture was not being recorded. At the end of my presentation, a woman my age approached me with some information scribbled on a yellow sheet of paper from a legal pad. She said, "My husband is a doctor, and I'm a nurse. My husband was recently diagnosed with prostate cancer. He did a great deal of research on the very best doctors in the nation and narrowed it down to those who have had the best results in successfully removing prostate cancer and giving their patients a full recovery. The doctor we found was right in our city of Austin, Texas. I've put the doctor's name on this paper, as well as our names and contact information. If you would ever consider this type of robotic surgery, and this location, we would be happy to have you stay with us for the mandatory ten-day recuperation before returning home to California."

She was an absolute stranger.

She obviously didn't know us at all, and frankly, I couldn't fathom staying one day, much less ten, with a stranger. More specifically, I knew that my husband was not open—at all—to robotic surgery for the removal of his prostate.

But I graciously took the yellow piece of paper and put it in the front pocket of my prayer notebook and flew home that night to California.

When Roger picked me up at the airport, I wasn't in the car two minutes before I said, "Hey, I know you haven't even considered robotic surgery as an option, but I met this lady from Austin, Texas, who told me about a doctor who had successfully removed her husband's prostate, and now he's cancer-free. The doctor's name is—"

Before I could finish the sentence, my husband finished it by saying the doctor's name. He was shocked.

He said, "Just today, someone told me about this doctor and his innovative procedure, and I researched it further. If my count goes up, I would actually consider it." I was shocked.

So I gave my husband the contact information from the woman I met at the end of the conference but kept the yellow piece of paper in the front pocket of my notebook.

We continued to pray daily and followed the "watch-and-wait" protocol until mid-December 2006, when my husband's PSA count suddenly jumped up over seven points.

The very day we got the news, we felt we had received our "marching orders" from God. I found the yellow paper and sent an email to Diane—whose voice and face I couldn't even remember. I asked her if my husband could contact her husband.

On December 28, 2006, my husband flew to Austin, and was picked up by Diane's husband, Denny—whom he had never met. Denny took my husband to meet with the doctor, who had, at very short notice, found time not only to meet with my husband, but to squeeze him in for an operation the following week.

Roger stayed at Denny and Diane's home that night, and Denny drove him back to the airport the next day.

Only a week later, Roger and I landed in Austin. He had the surgery, and we spent the following ten days in the home of these complete strangers—who ultimately became my husband's caretakers, our nightly dinner partners, our daily walking partners, and our friends. We left Texas in mid-January 2007 and returned home. I can't explain how I—a somewhat high-maintenance kind of gal—could feel as if I had been on a vacation or as if I had never left home, but that is how it felt to me. More important, Roger very quickly recovered from his operation—something he was concerned would be a much longer process—and has been cancer-free for over a year now. (He was also healthy enough to preside as a pastor at our son's wedding two months later.)

God talks. He does!

He nudges you to turn left or right, to talk or be silent. He encourages you to give and take, to stop or go. He whispers—and shouts—until He gets your attention. He makes His very specific ways known to you. He goes before and behind you.

Let God talk to you.

Let God Talk to You

God wants to talk to you. He desires to spend time with you, not just occasionally or when it is convenient, but every day of your life. Whatever the reason you picked up this book, God knew it would encourage you to develop your own personal, conversational relationship with Him and find within those conversations what I have found:

a safe oasis if you're wounded, rejected, or hurting;

a trustworthy accountability partner;

a counselor who knows you intimately;

an honest, forgiving, and holy God, whose wisdom and love you can depend upon.

Let God Talk to You

Put DOWN this book and decide the time and place you will meet with God *today*. Don't worry about next week, or next month, or the "what ifs." Just plan the "when and how" you will talk and listen to God before this day ends. And if you need a jump start, follow this pattern:

Find a quiet place. Take along paper, pen, and a Bible.

Intentionally turn yourself—heart, mind, and body—toward God and away from your world and its worries. Begin your two-way conversation in writing.

Tell God who He is to you—Father, Son, and Holy Spirit—and express your love for Him. Let God talk to you, telling you just how much He loves *you*.

Ask Jesus for forgiveness for anything that comes to mind. Then wait.

Let God wash over you with His purifying, cleansing Holy Spirit.

Ask the Holy Spirit for help or wisdom to address any present concern or need. Be specific. Let God talk to you by giving you thoughts and impressions of how He wants to move and work practically in your life.

Thank God for the most recent ways He has touched your life. Be specific.

Next, let God talk to you by opening the Bible to a psalm (Psalm 5 or 139, for starters) or to a chapter in one of the New Testament gospels (Matthew 6, Luke 11, or John 3, for example). Write down any verses in Scripture that give you immediate comfort, guidance, or correction. Commit one of the verses to memory—allowing God's Word to continue to speak to you throughout the coming days.

Then ask God if there is anything that you can do for Him. Be expectant—watching, listening, and waiting—for His answer. Record your very next thoughts or impressions *as well as your responses to God*. Date the page.

Finally, tell someone about your conversation with God—how you felt, what you heard, and what you are going to do next.

Why should you let God talk to you right now, today, and every day?

God waits for you.

He has so much to tell you.

No one loves you like God loves you.

But most of all, when you hear the living, loving God talk to *you,* you will never be the same.

ENDNOTES

Chapter 1: *God Talks to Anyone!*

1. Dallas Willard, *Hearing God* (Downers Grove, IL: InterVarsity, 1999), 222.

2. Catherine Marshall, *A Man Called Peter* (New York: McGraw-Hill, 1951), 304.

3. Ibid., 319.

Chapter 2: *Why God Talks to You*

1. Willard, *Hearing God,* 35.

2. Arthur T. Pierson, *George Müller of Bristol* (Old Tappan, NJ: Revell, 1899), 140.

3. Ibid., 178.

Chapter 3: *How God Talks to You*

1. A. W. Tozer, *The Knowledge of the Holy* (San Francisco: HarperSanFrancisco, 1961), 1.

2. Rosalind Rinker, *Prayer: Conversing With God* (Grand Rapids, MI: Zondervan, 1959), 33.

3. Eugene H. Peterson, *The Jesus Way* (Grand Rapids, MI:

Eerdmans, 2007), 264.

4. Ibid., 269.

5. Andrew Murray, *The Inner Life* (Grand Rapids, MI: Zondervan, 1980), 12.

6. H. A. Ironside, *I and II Timothy, Titus and Philemon* (Grand Rapids, MI: Kregel, 2008), 123.

7. Ibid., 123.

8. J. Oswald Sanders, *Spiritual Leadership* (Chicago: Moody Press, 1994), 82.

9. Oswald Chambers, *My Utmost for His Highest* (Grand Rapids, MI: Discovery House, 1992), 316, November 10.

10. Dietrich Bonhoeffer, *The Cost of Discipleship* (New York: Touchstone, 1995), 213.

11. Chambers, *My Utmost for His Highest,* 356.

Chapter 4: *What God Says When He Talks*

1. Dietrich Bonhoeffer, *Life Together* (San Francisco: HarperSanFrancisco, 1954), 115.

2. Ibid., 114.

3. I've changed this name to protect the identity of this young woman who shared her story with me.

4. Chambers, *My Utmost for His Highest,* 312.

Chapter 5: *When God Talks to You*

1. Chambers, *My Utmost for His Highest,* 350.

2. Willard, *Hearing God,* 219.

3. R. A. Torrey, quoted in Wesley L. Duewel, *Mighty Prevailing Prayer* (Grand Rapids, MI: Zondervan, 1990), 313.

4. Chambers, *My Utmost for His Highest,* 354.

5. Henri J. M. Nouwen, *The Way of the Heart* (San Francisco: HarperSanFrancisco, 1981), 31.

6. E. M. Bounds, *Purpose in Prayer* (New Kensington, PA: Whitaker House, 1997), 82.

7. Nouwen, *The Way of the Heart,* 69.

8. Murray, *The Inner Life,* 3–4.

9. Quoted in E. M. Bounds, *Purpose in Prayer,* 87.

10. Ibid., 88–89.

11. Earl O. Roe, *Dream Big* (Ventura, CA: Regal Books, 1990), 218–19.

12. V. Raymond Edman, *They Found the Secret* (Grand Rapids, MI: Zondervan, 1984), 58–59.

13. Michael Richardson, *Amazing Faith* (Colorado Springs: Waterbrook, 2000), 37, emphasis added.

14. Chambers, *My Utmost for His Highest,* 362, December 27.

Chapter 6: *Increase Your Desire for Hearing God Talk*

1. Rinker, *Prayer: Conversing With God,* 23.

2. Chambers, *My Utmost for His Highest,* 30, January 30.

3. Public domain, author unknown.

4. Willard, *Hearing God,* 218.

5. Rinker, *Prayer: Conversing With God,* 24–25.

6. Rick Warren, *The Purpose-Driven Life* (Grand Rapids, MI: Zondervan, 2002), 22.

7. Ibid., 25. A footnote in the book references Isaiah 46:3–4 (NCV).

8. Chambers, *My Utmost for His Highest,* 362, December 27.

Chapter 7: *Develop the Discipline of Hearing God Talk*

1. Nouwen, *The Way of the Heart,* 94.

2. Chambers, *My Utmost for His Highest,* 53, February 22.

3. R. A. Torrey, *How to Pray* (Springdale, PA: Whitaker House, 1983), 51.

4. Leonard Ravenhill, *Revival Praying* (Minneapolis, MN: Bethany House, 1962), 124.

5. R. A. Torrey, *The Power of Prayer* (Grand Rapids, MI: Zondervan, 1924), 28.

6. Willard, *Hearing God*, 201.

7. Richard J. Foster, *Freedom of Simplicity* (New York: HarperCollins, 1981), 105.

8. Chris Tiegreen, *Creative Prayer* (Colorado Springs: Multnomah, 2007), 150.

9. Ibid., 151.

10. Ibid., 100.

Chapter 8: *Have a Daily Design for "God Talks"*

1. Becky Tirabassi, *My Partner Prayer Notebook* (Newport Beach, CA: Becky Tirabassi Change Your Life, Inc.®, 1984, 1990, 2005, 2009).

2. Ibid.

3. Eugene H. Peterson, *Conversations: The Message With Its Translator* (Colorado Springs: NavPress, 2005), 773.

4. Ibid.

5. John Owen, *Sin and Temptation*, Dr. James M. Houston, ed. (Minneapolis, MN: Bethany House, 1996), 159–60.

6. William Wilberforce, *Real Christianity*, Dr. James M. Houston, ed. (Minneapolis, MN: Bethany House, 1997), 48.

7. O. Hallesby, *Prayer*, Clarence J. Carlsen, trans. (Minneapolis, MN: Augsburg Fortress, 1994), 153.

8. Quoted in E. M. Bounds, *Purpose in Prayer*, 70.

9. Jodie Berndt, *Praying the Scriptures for Your Children* (Grand Rapids, MI: Zondervan, 2001), 223.

10. Bonhoeffer, *Life Together*, 87.

11. Wesley L. Duewel, *Mighty Prevailing Prayer* (Grand Rapids, MI: Zondervan, 1990), 18.

12. Ibid., 21.

13. Ibid., 23.

14. Rueben P. Job and Norman Shawchuck, *A Guide to Prayer for Ministers and Other Servants* (Nashville: The Upper Room, 1983), 378.

15. Becky Tirabassi, *Change Your Life Daily Bible, Special Edition of The One-Year Bible, New Living Translation* (Wheaton, IL: Tyndale House, 1985, 1999).

ABOUT THE AUTHOR

Becky Tirabassi shares her dramatic life story every chance she gets, including in her books and venues such as the Greater Cleveland Billy Graham Crusade, *Focus on the Family, Enjoying Everyday Life with Joyce Meyer,* and Women of Faith. Becky's message resonates with people of all ages. She is the president of Becky Tirabassi Change Your Life, Inc., and founder of a non-profit student organization called Burning Hearts, Inc., issuing a counter-cultural call to be sold out to prayer, set apart in purity, and sent out with purpose. Her bestselling books include *Let Prayer Change Your Life, My Partner Prayer Notebook,* and the *Change Your Life Daily Bible.* Becky and her husband, Roger, live in Corona Del Mar, California.

To find out more about Becky Tirabassi, contact:

Change Your Life, Inc.
P.O. Box 9672
Newport Beach, CA 92660
1-800-444-6189 or 1-949-752-6855
Fax: 1-949-752-6830
www.changeyourlifedaily.com
www.beckytirabassi.com